Br

To my mother, with grateful
thanks for her support and
encouragement through the
years

# Breakout

Faith at work in today's society

## Val Howard

Inter-Varsity Press

**Inter-Varsity Press**
*38 De Montfort Street, Leicester LE1 7GP, England*

Unless otherwise stated, Scripture quotations in this publication are from the Holy Bible, New International Version. Copyright © 1973, 1978, 1984 International Bible Society. Published by Hodder & Stoughton.

*First published 1988*

**British Library Cataloguing in Publication Data**
Howard, Val
   Breakout: Faith at work in today's society
   1. Christian life
   I. Title
   248.4      BV4501.2

ISBN 0-85110-830-X

Typeset in Palatino by
Parker Typesetting Service, Leicester
Printed and bound in Great Britain by
Cox & Wyman Ltd, Reading

*Inter-Varsity Press is the publishing division of the Universities and Colleges Christian Fellowship (formerly the Inter-Varsity Fellowship), a student movement linking Christian Unions in universities and colleges throughout the United Kingdom and the Republic of Ireland, and a member movement of the International Fellowship of Evangelical Students. For information about local and national activities write to UCCF, 38 De Montfort Street, Leicester LE1 7GP.*

# Contents

# CHAPTER ONE

# You have Potential

The early morning mist that had shrouded the lower-lying areas of Kent finally rolled away. Ignoring the weather forecast completely, the sun was now streaming through the picture windows of the conference centre's main lounge. It was going to be a beautiful day – just the kind of day to put everyone in the right mood for a conference. I was surprised, therefore, to see Pauline still looking so glum. She had tried to join in the activities of the previous day but it was obvious that something was very wrong. This morning she looked close to tears.

'I feel a failure,' she finally confessed. 'I can't seem to find the balance between being a Christian and being a person. All the things I used to enjoy doing are wrong, and all the things I *should* do as a Christian I find so boring.'

I began to ask her more about herself. She had been a Christian for two years. Before that time she had had no church background and had led a happy-go-lucky life with the usual ups and downs of love affairs, job changes, ambitions and dreams. A very normal girl. After her conversion she got involved in a church and that's where her troubles began.

Realizing she should now be different, she began to do all the things she saw those around her doing and became more and more confused in the process. Well-meaning Christians, genuinely wanting to help, showered her with 'dos' and 'don'ts'. Her pathetic cry from the heart summed it up in four words, 'It just isn't *me*!' In those few short minutes I could see that far from being liberated as a Christian she had become bound to another slavemaster, legalism, and her natural spontaneity and sparkle were gone.

I fully realize that Pauline's case is somewhat extreme, but to some degree I think her experience is shared by all of us at some time in our lives. Becoming a Christian is a radical experience, or it should be, and it may involve a change of habits, conduct and life-style. But the end result should be greater depth, greater freedom and *more* sparkle, as we become what God wants us to be. The danger is that we tend to become slaves to what *others* think we should be.

I believe it is high time we Christians took a long, hard look at ourselves. Within the context of the world in which we live we need to look at our God-given potential to be what God intended us to be. Then we must draw on that potential, and learn to develop it into actions which will transform our lives and bring glory to the God who created us.

If we have surrendered our lives to Jesus Christ, then we are spiritually re-created beings. The apostle Paul explains very clearly what has happened to us: 'If anyone is in Christ, he is a new creation; the old has gone, the new has come!' (2 Corinthians 5:17). This is the miracle that transforms us and ensures that we can take our place with the risen Lord for ever. Yet for many of us the fact that 'the new has come' whilst we walk on the face of corrupted earth poses a major problem. We don't know what to do. We're not sure how to live. Spiritual beings we may now be, but our earthly bodies, with their senses, physical characteristics, desires and needs, are totally human (not to mention sinful). Suddenly we become aware of a conflict. We seek help from fellow Christians, but often find that they have the same problem.

The environment or culture in which we live is also completely alien to our new state, yet we must continue to live within it just like everyone else. Suddenly we begin to feel out of place.

## An odd one out

I remember in the days following my own conversion, looking around at the familiar streets of Manchester where I lived, watching the people I encountered day after day on buses and trains, reading the all-too-familiar daily newspaper reports of international and world affairs. It seemed strange that none of these things had changed as I had done. I knew something fundamental had happened to my very existence and spiritual identity. I knew beyond a doubt that I had undergone a radical transformation of soul and spirit, yet my surroundings remained unchanged. I began to realize, as I looked around me, that I was, in fact, an odd one out.

My new-found relationship with Jesus Christ had become extremely meaningful to me in a very short time. I had discovered that Jesus was alive and as real a person as any of my family or friends. Why, then, could they not understand? Surely it was crystal clear? It was to me. Why not to them also? And so it went on, the creeping sense of being different, even alienated, becoming stronger every day. I soon began to understand Jesus' words, 'They are not of the world, even as I am not of it' (John 17:16).

When someone becomes a Christian he becomes a square peg in a round hole. Finding the key to live as God wants us to live, in a world so foreign, is a constant battle. The temptation is to give in and become like everyone else, or to run away and hide. And yet if we look into the Scriptures we see that this battle is exactly where God wants us to be. Jesus spoke of being 'not of this world' as something we should experience whilst still in the world. Earlier in John 17 he prays to the Father, *not* that he should 'take them *out* of the world but that [he should] protect them from the evil one' (verse 15).

God wants us to be right where we are – in the thick of it. He has no intention of making things easier for us. 'In the battle' is the place in which he desires us to glorify him, by the way we think, live and act against the alien backdrop of a corrupt world.

## The strength in our frailty

Looking at it all from God's point of view and finding out what it means to 'walk in the Spirit', the conflict ceases to be a negative thing. It suddenly becomes a very *positive* thing, an opportunity to see the victory Christ died to give us in our daily lives.

However, we possess this treasure [the divine light of the gospel] in frail human vessels of earth, that the grandeur and exceeding greatness of the power may be shown to be of God and not from ourselves (2 Corinthians 4:7, Amplified).

Only through the frailty of our human frame, with all its vulnerabilities to the world around us, can the full extent of the dynamic, life-changing power of God begin to be fully realized. This incredible truth makes us unique. Not only unique as a body, the church of God, but also as individuals. It is this uniqueness which places us on a plane so vastly removed from human understanding that to the world we *are* strange. We *are* misguided – even laughable. We *are* the 'odd men out'. We *are* square pegs in a round hole. But what a challenge that places before us!

In the incredible wisdom of God's plan, we have been placed in a scenario in which we can blossom into the people he wants us to be.

Why, then, do so many of us never really see it this way? Fear, tradition, culture, background, even upbringing, can all stand in the way of a fuller understanding of our potential as Christians in this world which seems so alien and threatening. In what follows I hope to open up the areas that we often find so stifling – how we communicate, our emotions, our sexuality, the use of our minds. But first, why do Christians often appear so *colourless*?

# Christian Square Pegs

After a successful morning's shopping Chris and I found our way to a popular tea shop. As I was sitting there, savouring our perfectly brewed tea, Chris broke through my reverie. 'Do you know what I heard on the underground yesterday?' she asked. 'Two girls behind me on the platform were talking about Christians. One said to the other, "The trouble with Christians is that they are *colourless*".'

As the conversation continued we remembered other similar comments we had heard. 'Christians are boring', 'Christians don't seem to enjoy themselves'. . . . Over another cup of tea we tried to identify what it is that the world sees and calls colourless and boring, and we came to the conclusion that it had something to do with the Christian's difficulty in relating successfully to the world around him.

Having been freed by the blood of Christ from one kind of prison, that of sin without forgiveness, Christians can often dive headlong into another, the prison of legalism brought about by fear. Fear of sin. Fear of failure.

As I look at my own life and the constant battle I wage with the influences of the world around me, I notice that I often seek refuge in other Christians. I long for the fellowship and support of others who share my faith. This is a scriptural and right thing to do, but sometimes it is only an escape. In my desire to run away from the world's 'contamination', I fall into the trap of *isolating* myself from the world, living totally in the protected and cocooned culture of the church and my Christian friends. It is this kind of *isolated* Christian, I believe, that the world calls 'colourless'.

As the world appears to get nastier, Christians could be forgiven for thinking that the best way of dealing with the problem is to withdraw into the safety of their churches and fellowships. It seems logical to ask, 'Why battle as a square peg in the world when I can feel comfortable inside my fellowship group?' However, by withdrawing from the mainstream of life we remove ourselves from what is perhaps the most effective environment for victory over sin, the victory which ultimately brings glory to God.

It is only as we are forced to function in an alien environment that we begin to realize the extent of our own sin. We begin to see how dependent we are on God's mercy and forgiveness. We then begin to taste victory in areas of our lives we perhaps never knew existed. This, in turn, brings more glory to God. To miss this experience is nothing short of a tragedy. There is something very beautiful and genuine about a Christian who knows the depths of true forgiveness and repentance, and finds them working in practice, not just in the pages of his Bible.

## A liberated spirit

Part of that beauty is found in the attractiveness

of what I would call a 'liberated spirit'. Such a person is liberated from fear: fear of putting a foot wrong; fear of falling into sin. Such a person is confident in the faithfulness of the Holy Spirit to prompt him back into line, confident of God's forgiveness when he falls; and he is willing to pick himself up *by faith* and head back into the battle, because we have no prior *guarantee* of success.

I am convinced that fear is part of the reason why many Christians withdraw from the battle, even the fear of developing themselves as individuals lest they stand out as being different. We will look at this more closely in subsequent chapters. Or they are fearful of any involvement with those who do not know the Lord. They feel uncomfortable with them and so escape into the comparative comfort of their churches and fellowships.

The problem with all this is, of course, that the fear may push the person into a life-style, a pattern or mode of behaviour, which is very likely not his own. He will merely pick up from those around him that which makes him acceptable (or what he *thinks* makes him acceptable) to them and that which makes him feel comfortable and less fearful. And on top of all this he feels a sense of inadequacy in relating to the very people God has called him to reach.

But in talking about a 'liberated spirit' I am not advocating for one moment a life of abandonment and licence. What I am referring to is a life of dynamism and faith. Paul speaks out very strongly indeed against fearful and legalistic Christians. 'It is for freedom that Christ has set us free. Stand firm, then, and do not let yourselves be burdened again by a yoke of slavery' (Galatians 5:1). The Galatian Christians had fallen into the trap of trying to add works to their salvation. Grace was not enough for them. Paul goes on to explain his concern: 'You who are trying to be justified by law have been alienated from Christ; you have fallen away from grace. But by *faith* we eagerly await through the Spirit the righteousness for which we hope' (verses 4–5, italics mine).

Sensing the reaction of his readers to his letter, he clarifies the difference between legalism and licence. 'You, my brothers, were called to be free. But do not use your freedom to indulge the sinful nature; rather, serve one another in love' (verse 13). 'So I say, live by the Spirit, and you will not gratify the desires of the sinful nature' (verse 16). Note the New International Version's translation of verse 16: 'Live by the Spirit *and you will not . . .*' It would appear that Paul is saying that someone who is truly walking in the Spirit need not be afraid of stepping out of line. The Holy Spirit is faithful to prompt, because that person's heart is set on obedience by faith.

Walking in the Spirit means walking by faith. And walking by faith is only possible in the life of someone who is firmly grounded in the word of God. 'Faith comes from hearing the message, and the message is heard through the word of Christ' (Romans 10:17).

The fears and insecurities experienced by many Christians today come, to a large extent, as a result of a poor grasp of scriptural truth. If we have a daily and substantial intake of Scripture and are learning with increasing skill to apply its principles to our daily lives, then we will begin to form *convictions* about issues facing the world, our work, our country, our families. It is conviction based on the unchanging absolutes of Scripture, which gives us the foundation on which to form our life-style, make our decisions, develop our individual strengths. That makes us less dependent upon others to tell us what to do and how to do it. We become more dependent on God, who is then able to liberate us from legalism and fear. This in turn brings with it a confidence in God which is not only glorifying to him but makes us very attractive people.

If this is our experience, then God can and will do great things for us and through us. The daily grind of battling through a world without God suddenly takes on a new meaning, offering new challenges. In his excellent book, *Secular Work is Full-Time Service*, Larry Peabody pays particular attention to the role that the world can play in our spiritual development:

> As God forms Christ within us, He tests and tries us to be certain that the material measures up and that the work is being done thoroughly. Peter tells us that these trials and tests come 'that the proof of our faith, being more precious than gold which is perishable, even though tested by fire, may be found to result in praise and glory and honour at the revelation of Jesus Christ' (1 Peter 5:7) . . .
>
> Our occupations are often used as testing grounds. What attachments really hold our hearts? Does God enjoy the supreme

allegiance there? Or do the things of this world and our own bodies mean more to us? Through the adverse circumstances that God allows on the job, the answer to these questions will become clear ... How shall we view the daily grind? Perhaps we can compare it to the grinding of a lens. God wants to focus the light of the world through us and beam it into this world's darkness. But first He must shape the glass into an effective lens.

Our work can, if we allow it and recognise God's hand in it, be used to grind us, smooth us, polish us and fit us for the service of the Living God. Through the commonplace and humdrum circumstances of every day, we are given opportunity to die to self and live for Christ alone. We are broken, and we are tested. In it all, God wants to increase His light within us, then through us to concentrate His healing rays on others who live and work in Babylon.

(Larry Peabody: *Secular Work is Full-time Service* (CLC, 1974))

# Fear of over-identification

I am saddened when I hear of Christians who have totally opted out of life outside their protected environment. They may choose to have no friendships with anyone other than Christians. They read only Christian books. In fact, their only influences are Christian and they refuse to understand the world's thinking and its problems. I cannot count how many times people like this have said to me, 'It is dangerous to over-identify with the world. It is not helpful. We can fall into sin.' The same two points come up each time: 'over-identify' and 'fall into sin'.

First, never would I suggest that we 'over-identify' – only that we identify more effectively. Second, do such people ever consider the sin of legalism? Or the sin of refusing to walk by faith? Or even the sin of unwillingness to look at oneself and see if there is anything there which may be displeasing to God?

It is a common phenomenon among Christians to jump to extreme conclusions, to swing from one extreme of the pendulum to the other. Somehow it is difficult for us to find the balance.

It takes effort to develop a stable life based on scriptural conviction. It necessitates time in terms of study, personal devotional times alone with God and time to think out one's own individual character and personality. Many Christians don't know how or are simply not prepared to give time to that kind of effort and would rather spend it in the seemingly 'good' activities of church. The result is that when God does challenge them they are unable to respond in a biblical way. Our churches would be a whole lot healthier and far more able to deal with the issues of the world today if their individual members developed for themselves a stable and mature relationship with God.

There is a strong tide running the way of doing things together nowadays. This is better than the old-fashioned individualism, but there's a danger in feeling that we have no problems that a spot of worship can't solve. Get together with the saints, fling up some 'Hallelujahs' and all will be fine. But the cultivation of a personal devotional life matters as well. And that private devotional life must spread to the day-to-day conflicts of real living.

The conflict we face in our everyday lives offers us the vehicle by which we can become colour*ful* Christians. But we must come out of our hiding places and enter the daily battle. As that battle reveals what we are, and as we then progress to victory, the colours which will appear in our individual characters will reflect the glory of God.

CHAPTER · THREE

# The Christian Sub-culture

Sally became a Christian as a child through Sunday School. She grew steadily and as the years went by began to be concerned for people who did not share her faith. She began to talk to her colleagues about God and to pray regularly for their salvation. But as time went by, Sally's colleagues began to avoid her. They would talk behind her back: 'Sally can't talk about anything but religion. She's getting on my nerves!'

She did, in fact, lead someone to Christ and that person is going on well. But on the whole she did not stir up in her colleagues an interest in the blessings and riches found only in Christ. She positively, or rather, negatively, put them off!

John, on the other hand, told me about someone he works with who one day accidentally let slip that he was a Christian. John said to me: 'I would never have known. Had he not said by chance, "I once committed my life to God", there's absolutely no reason why I should have ever thought that. He's no different from the rest of us.' He sounded a little disappointed and when I questioned him further he said, 'Well, Christianity is supposed to offer us something, but I don't see anything different in his life. What's he got that I haven't?'

These are two obvious extremes and there are

of course many exceptions. But if we are truly honest, these two examples reflect the state of much Christian witness today.

The conflict of living a life pleasing to God in an alien environment naturally spills over into our communication. The pendulum often swings between the 'holier than thou' type of Christian who cannot communicate with people in the world (except to bore them) and the Christian who identifies so much with the world that there's nothing different about him. To the unbeliever he has nothing to offer.

We have already discussed the fact that the world seems to be getting nastier. Perhaps part of the reason for this is that the values and standards society once held as virtues to be striven for are gradually disappearing. One by one, Christian values have been discarded as irrelevant to today's needs. They are out of date.

Twenty years ago it was much easier to talk to people directly about Christ. They still had some framework, some background to which they could relate the things that Christians may have said to them. Now, that framework has been chipped away and it's getting harder for the world to relate to the values and principles of Scripture.

The gap between the church and the world is widening all the time and the sad thing is that many of us Christians cannot or will not recognize it. We will not admit to our own responsibility to build the necessary bridges across the gap. Instead we withdraw further into our fellowships to ensure a safe distance between ourselves and corruption, but thereby cutting ourselves off from possible friendships with unbelievers, from the vital first-hand experience we must have in order to meet their needs.

Jim Petersen puts it very clearly in his book *Evangelism as a Lifestyle*. He tells of a seminar he attended in which the lecturer said:

'As a Christian takes his stand, he forces his non-Christian friends and acquaintances to choose. They will either be drawn into the Christian life or they will withdraw. Withdrawal also means loss of friendship. Consequently, there will come a time when the maturing Christian has no real friendships among non-Christians.' Another speaker at the same seminar said: 'As we become more and more mature, we become less and less effective with the world.'

Is this what we mean by a safe distance? To think it is a Christian virtue to have no real friendships with unbelievers? If we do, that is tragic because such isolation has a destructive effect on a local body of Christians as well as destroying our communication with the lost. Christians who keep to themselves, who do not experience a continuing influx of people just arriving from the dominion of darkness, soon surround themselves with their own sub-culture. Receiving no feedback from people fresh from the world, they forget what it is like to be out there. Peculiar language codes, behavioural patterns and communication techniques emerge that only have meaning for the insiders. As such a local body becomes increasingly ingrown. It also

becomes stranger and stranger to outsiders.
Eventually communication with the man on
the street is impossible.

(Jim Petersen: *Evangelism as a Lifestyle* (NAV-PRESS, 1980))

## Sub-culture

So in trying to combat the influences and contamination of a decaying world, we Christians tend to isolate ourselves from the very world which God has sent us to reach. And it is this 'sub-culture' which the world sees and mistakes for Christianity. What they actually see is a caricature of the real thing. Within the protective bubble of our own culture, we become ignorant of the world's thinking. We don't know what makes it tick any more and therefore we are like foreigners to the unbelieving world, and unbelievers are like foreigners to us.

But if the problem is great among those Christians who are in secular jobs, surrounded by unbelievers all day and every day, how much greater is it for those who by the nature of their work are removed from this daily, natural exposure to the world? I speak from personal experience.

For nine years I worked full time for a Christian organization in both Britain and Europe. During that time, I thought of myself as one who demonstrated a 'balanced life' and who could therefore relate well to unbelievers. But then I learned hard and bitter lessons through the transition from full-time Christian work into a secular environment.

As a Christian worker of course I met many unbelievers through the organized evangelism that we did, through the working Christians who were living with me and through contact with my neighbours. I didn't feel particularly uncomfortable with them and occasionally wondered why so much fuss was made about the problem of 'identifying with the world'.

The answer to that came when, after nine years in an environment in which all my colleagues were Christians, I went back to a secular job in a highly competitive industry. The shock was incredible. It is no exaggeration to say that during that first year I wondered if I was going to survive. So much for the confident full-timer who thought she handled the world's influences well and related easily to the world! I realized with horror how cocooned I had been in Christian work. In truth, I had no idea of what the real world was all about. My experience had been second-hand. In my contact with neighbours and in organized evangelism, the relationship with unbelievers had always been under my control and on my terms. In a secular job I was thrust into their world on their terms.

Since then I have talked to many friends who are working in a full-time Christian environment. Some have said to me, 'It's good to be living with Christians who have ordinary jobs. It keeps you in touch with the world, and so does organized evangelism.' These things certainly help but (and I say this with love and respect for all my many friends who are in full-time Christian work) their experience can only ever be, at best, second-hand. It is only as we are constantly exposed to the ordinary everyday life of the unbeliever in his work, in his own environment, that we really fully appreciate his mentality.

I am always thrilled to hear of full-time Christian workers who are taking steps to develop themselves in this area, immersing themselves in a secular environment for a significant period of time. It is possible to enrol in full-time courses, to mix with people who do not know the Lord and to get first-hand exposure. Work in a factory, on a building site, in a hospital, a shop or some kind of conservation project – all these are openings that might be explored. There *are* plenty of jobs going, even outside London, if you're prepared to do the ones that no-one else wants.

Christian organizations might well consider sending their long-term staff on 'refresher courses' of this kind, to imbibe a dose of real life. In the long run, it is an investment. It must be.

In the context of work or study, the Christian is placed on the same level as his unbelieving counterparts. In the day-to-day busyness, attitudes are tested and relationships become strained. To the unbeliever this is all part of life's rich pattern. He thinks nothing of it. For the Christian, if he is truly wanting to develop, it is a spiritual battle, not so much to remain obedient at the height of some irritation or disagreement (he can experience that with Christian colleagues too!) but to contend with his own human reactions to the kind of discourtesy, personal attack, immoral behaviour and general 'secular' pressure which only comes in an everyday unbelieving environment. So it is more than pure 'knowledge' the full-timer needs. He must have first-hand exposure; he must make himself vulnerable to the world. Not 'of' it, but 'in' it, he will then, and only then, fully appreciate how immense the problem is of relating to the lost. I wish I had thought of taking a break from my full-time involvement. If I had, I know I would have done many things differently on return to full-time ministry and I would have been much the richer for the experience.

## Inappropriate 'witness'

We can discuss techniques and styles of witness until the cows come home, but unless they are tested in the fire of the world we will lack sadly in effectiveness. Just as the world often sees a caricature of what a Christian is, so we often see in our mind's eye a caricature of what an unbeliever is. And so, led by this image, we say the things we *think* a Christian ought to say to such a person, simply because we cannot, or dare not, find out for ourselves what he really thinks. The results can be disastrous.

I remember one embarrassing incident when (while still a full-time Christian worker) I went out to buy a new skirt. A young Christian whom I had been helping said that she would come with me. I thought this was an ideal opportunity to show her how to witness 'naturally'. So I prayed for an opportunity.

We went into a shop and I saw just the skirt I had been looking for. The only trouble was that it cost more than I had intended to pay. The sales assistant looked as though she had a very heavy hangover. Either that, or she hadn't slept a wink the night before. Or she'd had a row with her boyfriend. Whatever her problem was, she certainly was wishing me miles away from her shop. I said to her, 'I really can't make up my mind. It's a little bit more than I intended to pay.' This didn't help her mood at all, and she scowled at me angrily. I went merrily on. 'I will go away and think about it and then I'll come back.' She shrugged her shoulders at this indecisive customer and walked away.

My friend and I went and had a cup of coffee and while we were sitting there I prayed about whether I should buy the skirt. Feeling happy about it, we went back to the shop. The sales assistant saw me coming and the scowl reappeared. It didn't seem to help her when I said that I was going to take the skirt after all. As she was wrapping it up, I thought, 'This is my opportunity! This is how I can show my young Christian friend how to proclaim Christ naturally.' So I said to the sales girl in my most 'natural' voice, 'I don't suppose you get many customers who pray before they buy a skirt, do you?' She stopped wrapping the skirt, looked me straight in the eye and said with a resigned expression on her face, 'You would be surprised. We get all sorts of weird people in here!'

Well, my 'witnessing' lesson was over for that day. A beautiful example of doing what I thought a Christian *ought* to do in a situation, instead of using my common sense and the brain that God, in his wisdom, had given me. I also felt a complete idiot in front of my young Christian friend.

My years in full-time work cushioned me from some of the sharp end of life, and what I believed to be typical of the world was nothing of the kind. Returning to a secular job, of course I wanted to witness. I wanted people to know that I was a Christian, and yet as time went on I found that although I wanted to say things about the Lord, whatever I said seemed inappropriate. The things that I thought would be applicable from my knowledge of the world and my knowledge of witnessing as I had learned it, seemed either totally inappropriate when it came to the crunch, or grossly mistimed.

I remember one incident with a colleague. My company was going through the consequences of the recession and things were looking quite bleak. I was concerned, as were all my colleagues, and I began to pray for a recovery. As time went on, the outlook seemed brighter. Sales took on a more healthy appearance and the company became much stronger. A colleague and I were talking about this one day. He said how pleased he was to hear about a new contract which had just been signed. Thinking this was an ideal opportunity to draw God into the conversation, I said to him, 'Yes, it is good, and do you know, I actually prayed for that to happen!'

My colleague swung round on me quite violently. He looked angry and his eyes flashed. He said, 'Who the hell do you think you are?' I gulped. In the previous nine years my Christian colleagues had never said anything like that to me! I said, 'What do you mean?' He said, 'Do you think that this company's success depends on the prayers of the likes of you?' I didn't know what to say. In a sense I suppose it *could* 'depend on my prayers', but seeing things from his point of view,

I must have sounded terribly pious and self-righteous.

Later on that day I went to him and apologized. He agreed that I had sounded self-righteous and pious but he slapped me on the shoulder and said, 'Never mind, you're OK', and got on with his work. I breathed a sigh of relief and determined there and then to learn a lesson from that.

What I had told him was appropriate to what he had said to me but my timing was way, way out of line. If I had used my head instead of my idea of 'what a Christian should do in a situation like that', I would have known that he would react violently. He is that type of man. He has no Christian background at all, so how could I possibly expect him to understand? I was the foolish one. I handled it badly.

We must get our act together and develop a healthy and mature relationship with God, using the world's backdrop to prime and shape us into whole people who can *reach* out to others. People will never be reached by aliens. We must do this both as individuals and corporately, or our impact on the world will diminish until there is nothing left to say. As that gap between the world and the church gets wider, so the group of people who might just respond to our bumbling witness gets smaller and smaller. Our responsibility is to find the common ground and to build the bridges. If we don't, even those whom we may lead to Christ will face the same dilemmas and the vicious circle will continue.

# Be natural

I have heard many a sad tale of someone who has become a Christian from a very worldly background and finds the new 'Christian world' unattractive and stifling. Well-meaning, caring Christians swamp them with Bible verses, with things they should now do, or not do, as young Christians, and draw them quickly into the fellowship of a church or Christian group. These are all good things in themselves, but often these young Christians turn away in fear because they feel so very foreign in the new world they have been introduced to. It's a strange thing, but the Christian 'sub-culture' and all that that means to us soon becomes second nature. We don't realize how strange we seem to the unbelieving world and we often take neither the blame nor the responsibility. We say things like, 'Well, if the world doesn't understand, it is because it is a sinful world'. We seem unable to take an honest look at ourselves, both as individuals and as a corporate body, lest we find some blame there. We must accept the fact that we communicate what we *are*. If we have never learned how God can enrich our lives through our obedience by faith in all kinds of circumstances then we will communicate an unnatural life.

I would like to quote again from Jim Petersen's book, *Evangelism as a Lifestyle*:

Now what does this matter of congruence, that is harmony with God's ways, have to do with reaching the unreachable? It has a great deal to do with it. A congruent life is the secret of naturalness in communication and naturalness is the secret of attracting rather than repelling with our witness. On the other hand where there are incongruities in our lives we usually have to resort to devices or gimmicks to get our message across.

We need to keep in tune with God and with our fellowships in order to develop the kind of communication which will be effective in the world. By turning too much the other way we will fail and will resort to gimmicks which the unbeliever will pick up straight away and will see through as a sham.

Since returning to a business environment it never ceases to amaze me how much money companies are prepared to spend every year to ensure that they present a positive image to the outside world. A good and positive image in the market place is one of the foremost objectives that any company can have. It is vital to its survival. Organizations spend millions of pounds on marketing and market research so that they know what the market's needs are and how their company can meet those needs.

What kind of attention do we give, as the corporate body of Christ, to our image? Do we know what kind of image we are presenting to the unbelieving world? And do we care? If we know, what are we doing to improve it? How much thought are we giving to that? How well informed are we about our 'market place'? Do we know how people are thinking? Do we know what our market's needs are? Are we aware of the ever-changing face of the world and its ever-changing mentalities? Do we know how to adjust our 'product' in order to meet those needs?

I am not, of course, saying that we should construct a false image which will hide what we really are. The exact opposite in fact. We communicate what we are and we are individuals with a wealth of potential and opportunities to be the kind of people who attract others to Jesus Christ. We should major on that. Be ourselves and let Christ have freedom to use us as we are, real human beings.

# CHAPTER FOUR

# Treasures in Jars of Clay

'You are a chosen people, a royal priesthood, a holy nation, a people belonging to God, that you may declare the praises of him who called you out of darkness into his marvellous light. Once you were not a people, but now you are the people of God; once you had not received mercy, but now you have received mercy' (1 Peter 2:9–10).

This passage of Scripture motivates me to be my best for God. According to Peter, I am chosen. I am part of a Royal Family. I am somebody. I have received mercy from the hand of God, the King of Kings.

As we think about developing ourselves in the alien environment of the world around us, it is this kind of truth which we need to grasp and believe. Fears, inhibitions and threat of legalism should melt into insignificance as we accept for ourselves each of these aspects of what we are in Christ.

If I am really the child of the King of Kings and part of a royal priesthood then surely my life should reflect that. What I am should infiltrate what I do and how I behave. In all facets of my life, and that includes the very important part of my life called my humanity.

When someone becomes a Christian he

embarks on a whole new way of life. He learns to pray, to study and apply Scripture, how to develop a devotional relationship with God and the qualities which please him. We could call this, for want of a better word, the 'spiritual' side of the Christian's life. God has made us stewards of our lives and in doing the things mentioned above we are exercising stewardship over our 'spirituality'. But similarly, God has also made us stewards of 'the other' side of our lives – our humanity, our lives in the human sense. Why is it that so many Christians seem to forget that they are people – human beings? Yes, our bodies are sinful. Yes, they can get in the way of so-called 'spiritual' progress. But the fact remains that God has ordained that we should live within these vehicles of our humanity until the day we are finally released from them. So, alongside the development of our 'spiritual' life we should be developing our 'human' life – not our sinfulness, to be sure, but the individual richness that makes us people.

I am always thrilled to think of the fact that Jesus is a man in heaven. He came to earth as a man and now, in heaven, it is the man Jesus Christ who sits at the right hand of God (Mark 16:19). Knowing that helps me to accept my own humanity. If God had intended that we should leave our human frame behind the moment we became Christians, then he would have made provision for that. Instead, he tells us to wait until the day, known only to him, on which we shall be released and transformed.

We are, then, created to be whole people, spiritually and humanly whole. Sometimes we are confused because we draw an unhelpful distinction between the two sides of our life. We talk about things being either 'spiritual' or 'secular'. But if we are Christians our life is, *in its entirety*, spiritual. Everything which touches me, whether it be the world, my family, or the everyday toil of my job, is a spiritual issue, simply because I am a spiritually re-created being. Therefore everything, including my own humanity, takes on a spiritual dimension. If we do not understand this, then there will be areas of our lives which will remain untouched and therefore undeveloped. We will not have experienced the life-changing power of God in them and therefore the potential for our glorifying God will be limited.

## Six key areas

I have chosen just six areas of our lives to look at more closely. Of course there are many more. But these are, I believe, some of the major 'human' areas which we often neglect but which, when consecrated, help develop us into whole people. They are all parts of our make-up which we find difficult to cope with to a greater or lesser degree, and yet they are all keys to the process of growth and development. For example, we often have problems in knowing what to say and when to say it and so I have chosen *speech* as a key area. In our *emotions* we often don't know how to deal with the things we feel. We can be led by them or we can ignore them altogether. How can we glorify God through our emotions?

Or take the *mind*. How much of our mind should be given to the word of God? How much

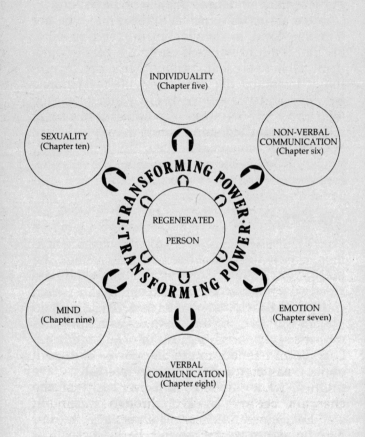

INDIVIDUALITY
(Chapter five)

SEXUALITY
(Chapter ten)

NON-VERBAL
COMMUNICATION
(Chapter six)

TRANSFORMING POWER · TRANSFORMING POWER

REGENERATED

PERSON

MIND
(Chapter nine)

EMOTION
(Chapter seven)

VERBAL
COMMUNICATION
(Chapter eight)

should we be thinking about the issues of the day, or politics? How much should we concentrate on developing our opinions and convictions about current affairs and about world concern?

These are what some call 'grey' areas. We are not sure what to do with them. And as often happens with grey areas, we tend either to push them to one side or to ignore them. Yet each of these facets of our humanity offers dynamic potential to see God's power at work. Once the Holy Spirit infiltrates areas like these we are going to become very different people indeed. Because the potential is so great I believe Satan will do his utmost to keep them grey and poorly defined in order to undermine our relationship with God and our effectiveness with others.

Looking at the illustration opposite, you will see that the central circle represents the regenerated person. The new creation, the born-again Christian. If everything is working perfectly then the power generated in that central core should pass along the channels to each of the individual areas shown. The result is a life which is pleasing and glorifying to God and which communicates through all its facets because the Holy Spirit has been given freedom to exercise power in each of them. It has truly become an integrated life.

Often what happens, however, is that the channels become blocked through misunderstanding, ignorance, fear. The result is that our lives appear to be unbalanced. Parts of our lives are not surrendered to the power of God. It is only as we make ourselves vulnerable that God can do his work. In chapter 1 I made reference to that great passage in 2 Corinthians 4:7: 'However, we possess this precious treasure, the divine light of the gospel, in frail human vessels of earth, that the grandeur and exceeding greatness of the power may be shown to be of God and not from ourselves' (Amplifed Bible). Our 'frailty' comes in all kinds of shapes and sizes. Upbringing, background, race, nationality, fears, insecurities, or just plain old sin could all be gathered under the umbrella of human frailty.

Our objective, surely, is that as we make ourselves vulnerable, the power of God would be shown through these human frailties. Trusting him to show the perfection of his power in these vital areas of our lives is an unmatched experience.

## Power in weakness

Perhaps one of the most wonderful truths for the Christian is that, in Christ, we are perfect. In God's sight we are holy, blameless and totally forgiven; we have been made new. When he looks at us, he looks at Christ and sees his perfection. But as long as we are on this earth that perfection is housed in 'frail human vessels of earth'. It is through faith that we take the truths that are ours to claim in Scripture and apply them to that human frailty. It is through the word of God that his power is brought into being as we claim each truth in quiet trust that God will make it a reality in our lives.

I mentioned earlier the 'grey' areas, and said that often our response to grey areas is to push them aside or to ignore them altogether. But another alternative is that we take each one, and bring it into the spotlight of scriptural truth. The reason why we have our treasures in an earthen vessel is, according to the verse in 2 Corinthians, 'so that the power may be shown to be of God and not from ourselves'.

I remember as a child reading a story about Ali Baba and the forty thieves. There was a picture in my book of forty thieves hiding in large eastern jars. The picture showed forty jars with a pair of eyes peeping over the top of each jar. That illustrates to me what many of us do. We accept the fact that our perfection in Christ is housed in frail human vessels of earth, but instead of trusting God to show his power in that frailty, instead of rising to his level of understanding and action, we try to bring God within the confines of our vessels, of our humanity. We limit him. We try to squeeze him into the space between ourselves and the inside of our jar. We ask him to help us to 'cope with our lot'. So we stay in the jar and take no risks.

What God is teaching us in that verse is that we are to draw on his power to break out of the frailty of our humanity. That his power will be made perfect in our existing weakness.

I am not a nuclear physicist but I am told that when two atoms fuse in a given set of circumstances, a vast amount of energy is released. I like to think of one atom being our human frailty. The other atom I like to thing of as being God's power available to us through his word. The fusion of those two units results in tremendous energy. God is glorified and we begin to communicate something which the world cannot deny. Instead of being Christians trying to 'live the Christian life' we become God-made people because his power is living *through our human frailty*. A life like that is a life which is living reality.

The trouble is, of course, that none of us likes to admit weakness. Society has conditioned us to believe that weakness is a bad thing. It can lead to failure. Society tells us that success is the thing that we should be aiming for. As Christians we understand that this is not God's way but nevertheless we are so contaminated by the world's thinking that even in our walk with God, success and failure are still two very emotive words.

We must begin by admitting what we are without Christ. We are nothing. We deserve nothing but hell. We have no rights. We have nothing that we can offer to God. The Bible says that 'all our righteous acts are like filthy rags' (Isaiah 64:6). So there we have it – we are nothing. If that were not true then it would not have been necessary for Jesus to come and die and rise again for us. And yet, amazingly, we have great difficulty in accepting the fact that outside of Christ we have nothing and are nothing. But it is a truly liberating experience if we can recognize that fact and then thank God for it. 'Lord, I am nothing. I know that I cannot do anything of myself to please you. How I need you.'

There is an interesting paradox here, however. There are many people who would readily admit that they are nothing and have nothing to offer. But instead of being humble, they despise themselves. I once knew of someone whose opinion of himself was so low that he actually detested the sight of himself in the mirror.

But this is a very different attitude from the one

I describe above. This kind of person is caught in the trap of thinking that there is no hope for him. He is beyond the reach of God. Such a person may feel that it is futile to 'be himself' because 'himself' is so totally unacceptable. However, what he may consider to be his true self and what God considers that to be are two very different things. God looks at us through the perfection of Christ and sees what we will become within the framework of our own self. Certainly we are nothing of ourselves, but what we become through the power of God is not 'more of our detestable and unacceptable self' but the person God created us to be.

How often do you hear Christians say, 'I'm sure God can't use me. I have so many weaknesses'? Then others say, 'But God can use you in spite of your weaknesses.' I would like to go a step further than that and say, 'God will use you *because* of your weaknesses.' Paul was someone who was convinced about this. In 2 Corinthians 12 he explains how God said to him, 'My grace is sufficient for you, for my power is made perfect in weakness.' And Paul goes on to say, 'I will boast all the more gladly about my weaknesses, so that Christ's power may rest on me. That is why, for Christ's sake, I delight in weaknesses, in insults, in hardships, in persecutions, in difficulties. For *when I am weak, then I am strong*' (verses 9–10).

However strong an individual may feel humanly, in God's sight he is weak. If we really look at the truth of these verses we see that the whole aspect of failure and success must be turned back to front.

# Called not to cope but to obey

When I think I am strong humanly, then I am in fact weak. But when I acknowledge my weaknesses honestly, then I have the potential to be very, very strong indeed. So much of our human frailty is pushed aside and hidden under what we would consider to be our human strengths. We can't bear to face the fact that we are in some areas less than strong. Sometimes Satan has us so bound by these things that we actually become very upset and distressed even to think of them. And so, consequently, they are never brought into the spotlight of scriptural truth. They are never dealt with. They are never laid at the cross, and God's grace and power are never claimed for those things. In those areas God remains unglorified and the world is robbed of example and witness. We are there in our 'eastern jars', unable to see over the rim, and that is exactly where the devil wants us to be. He has us by the throat – ineffective, frustrated and defeated.

Nowhere in Scripture does God call us to 'cope'. God calls us to *obedience* and in that obedience, by faith, he promises victory. And I believe that if we are not victorious, if we are not rising above human frailty, if God's power is not a living reality in that frailty, then we are missing unnumbered riches of experiences with God. Also, this lack of faith in our own lives will be projected to the lives of other Christians. If we cannot believe God that he will give us victory in our own lives, we will never be able to believe him for victory in the lives of others.

There are of course reasons for the weaknesses

that each of us may have. But there are no excuses. How often have you heard someone say, 'He has that problem because of a very difficult relationship he had many years ago'? Or, 'She's been that way ever since she took that difficult job'? Or again, 'You should meet her parents, then you'd understand why she's like that!'? In making excuses for ourselves, we make excuses for others. We are in fact excusing sin. If we have come to know Christ personally and the Spirit of the living God is therefore living within us, then although there may be many reasons for the way we are, there isn't one excuse. We are free to change.

God's power can be made perfect in all of those areas of our lives that we consider to be weak. When we excuse weakness and sin, we are watering down the gospel. We are dishonouring God. Until we learn to see our frailty as something we can thank God for and see his power at work in us, our impact on others' lives is going to be limited.

If ever there was a group of people limited by lack of education, low social standing, emotional instability, doubtfulness and the rest, then it was the twelve disciples to whom Jesus entrusted his ministry. It is surely not by accident that he chose twelve simple men to ensure that the ministry which he had begun on earth would continue according to his plan and requirements after he had returned to the Father. The fact that these men had very obvious limitations is a very significant factor in Jesus' plan. It was his intention that after the Holy Spirit came upon them they would be demonstrating a powerful life – power which was to become active in their limitations.

God's power, then, is shown up best in weak people. And we can draw on that power through holding on to the truth of Scripture, the absolutes of God's word. These things will never change. They are promises for all time. We have the victory. We are perfect in God's sight. We are forgiven. We are accepted in the Beloved. God is a righteous judge. He is holy. He does want the best for my life because he loves me. Truths such as these cannot be argued with. We must take them literally and we must bring our human frailty into the spotlight that shines from them. God will use us, not in spite of, but *because* of our weakness. He has chosen 'frail human vessels of earth' to communicate his power. It is a perfect plan and it was created in his infinite wisdom. Who are we to argue with him?

I remember a good friend telling me many years ago that he had decided to thank God for his weakness. He had listed all the things he considered to be standing in the way of a powerful life and, one by one, had brought them to the cross, asking God to show his power in each one to make him a stronger but God-made man. The change was remarkable. My friend's life was transformed during the years that followed and he is now a fine, godly and attractive man with an exceptionally fruitful ministry.

There is hope for every-one of us. There is potential in every one of us. In the following chapters we will look in more detail at the six areas of our make-up and identify ways in which that potential can be released.

# You are Unique

Some years ago I visited a large exhibition in the south of Holland. The purpose of the exhibition was to show man's social and technological development through the years. I was very impressed with the creativity with which the exhibition had been put together and the way the various stages of man's development were demonstrated.

After I had been wandering around for an hour or so, I came across a section which I hadn't noticed before. There was a model of a baby lying on a blanket. Above it was a light which flashed approximately every 1½ seconds. I read the explanatory board next to the exhibit. It said, 'Every 1½ seconds, a baby is born somewhere in the world.' A baby born every 1½ seconds! As I stood there looking at the model and the flashing light, I thought of Psalm 139, and was reminded of the verses which describe the intricacy and the design and the care with which each one of us is made: 'My frame was not hidden from you when I was made in the secret place. When I was woven together in the depths of the earth, your eyes saw my unformed body. All the days ordained for me were written in your book before one of them came to be' (Psalm 139:15–16). Every 1½ seconds a unique individual is created. Nowhere in the world will there be another quite like this one.

Our uniqueness is a difficult concept to grasp when we think of the vastness of the world's population today. Yet when we look at it from God's point of view, then we see that he would naturally want the relationship with each of his children to be unique. My relationship with God is very different from yours. And your relationship with God is very different from your neighbour's. If God created us individually with our own uniqueness, then it is surely dishonouring to him when we wish that we were someone else.

How many times have you thought, 'I wish I was like so and so . . . I wish I could do that as well as he can'? God has made you the way he wanted you to be because he wanted a certain kind of relationship, the kind he could have only with you the way you are. If you were someone else you would not relate to God in the way he desires.

We do often choose someone whom we feel is more acceptable and try to be like them, but if we do that then our own individuality and uniqueness will never be revealed, either to ourselves or to others. A whole wealth of riches, of strengths, even of weaknesses, which God is wanting to use for his glory, will be totally and utterly wasted. The you that God intended you to be will never be seen. If we remind ourselves of the illustration of the six circles, then I suppose I could suggest that individuality is actually wrongly placed. Perhaps instead of being a circle in its own right, it should be drawn as a concentric circle surrounding that central core. I say this because as we grow in Christ and those other areas are being developed, the process bears the colour of our individuality. You could say that the Holy Spirit's working in our lives passes through the screen of our individuality before it gets to those other areas. However I have placed individuality where it is simply because we very often neglect it.

## Examine your gifts

One of the most wonderful things about being an individual is that we have individual strengths and talents and gifts. I remember meeting a young man once who, in many areas of his life, was limited. He was often socially ill at ease and did not find it easy to relate to others. As he gradually became involved in his church, he was asked if he could perhaps do something in the church's Sunday school. Today that young man is the head of his church's Sunday school operation, and is a very gifted communicator to children as well as a child evangelist. A strength that he never knew he had was brought out and developed by God.

What often happens in a case like this is that because of the confidence gained in a new area, the person will therefore be bolder in addressing other needy areas. The chain reaction is very significant. It requires faith to sit down and ask God to show us what our strengths and our gifts are. It is much easier either to assume we have many gifts and get on with what we believe is our job, or to think that we don't have any gifts or strengths at all and try to merge into the background. Neither one of these options could ever be pleasing to God. We surely must look honestly and prayerfully at the person God has made us and ask him to develop that uniqueness through building on our gifts and our strengths and claiming his power in our weaknesses.

One of the greatest threats to the continued development of our individuality can be a heavy involvement in organized ministry. By that I do not mean that organized ministry is wrong, far from it. But it is possible to fall into the trap of thinking that the only way to serve God is to do what other Christians do in taking on activity after activity in the church.

I am often horrified at the speed at which some churches draw their very young converts into every activity they can possibly fit into their time after work. A young Christian will take on some responsibility because he feels that God is asking him to do that. This may be right, of course, and God most certainly does call people into the responsibilities of church life. But there is a danger in drawing young Christians in too much and too soon to the point that their life with God consists only of church activity. They have no time left for their unbelieving friends, their ready-made ministry; and they are carrying responsibility for helping others without spending sufficient time developing themselves.

Some years ago, while I was in full-time Christian work, I went through a crisis which I feel was partly brought on because I was giving so much of my energies and my time to 'ministry', that I neglected the development of my own individuality. The load I was carrying in my ministry was very heavy, and by the time I was finally ordered to rest by my doctor I was extremely tired. But I do believe that part of the burden I felt, and that finally brought me to a halt, was that I had been striving to be what I believed was a 'good leader' – someone who would give all their time and all their efforts to caring for their ministry. What I had in fact done was give what I did not have. It is impossible to be a true leader if there is no real person behind that leadership. In an effort to develop my leadership skills, I had squashed the person that was 'me'. I remember telling a friend that I felt that the real me was just a tiny, shrivelled cinder – dried out and totally incapable of communicating itself. Only when I realized this before God and began bit by bit to develop the real me, did I obtain peace again.

I sat down and thought of the things that I enjoyed doing and the strengths that I thought I had. I wrote down the things that I would like to do, areas I felt I would like to develop, but had never had the time to give to them. From these lists I selected just a few actions that I thought I could take in order to begin to develop 'me'. I decided to give time each day to one of these projects. I would spend some time with music, either playing my piano or listening to some favourite records or reading about a favourite composer. Other days I would select something else and really make an effort not only to enjoy doing these things but also to become more knowledgeable or more skilful in doing them. I then began to look at my career and how I could develop myself in that. In addition to all of this I began to discuss, on a much deeper level, all

kinds of issues and subjects with people of dif-
fering opinions and backgrounds. This stimulated
my thinking and as I prayerfully examined the
issues I had discussed, I discovered that I was
forming some strong opinions and views of my
own, sometimes very different from those I had
thought a Christian should have. As time went
on, I began to develop some individuality. I
found that I had strengths I had not previously
recognized, and as the months and years followed, I was thrilled to see how God began to use
some of these things to minister to other Christians and to improve my communication with
those without Christ.

## Be the real you

To look hard at ourselves does require faith and
imagination. In looking and accepting what we
see through the eyes of God and his forgiveness
and then thanking him for the way he has made
us, we begin to discover the tremendous potential
at our disposal to bring glory to God and to communicate the living reality of a God-made person.
This can only happen if we fully see and accept
the person God made us. Who we really are. To
do that takes prayer, time, the understanding and
love of others to help us to see where our
strengths lie and where our uniqueness shows up
best.

Perhaps one of the greatest enemies we have in
the fight to be ourselves is the fear of rejection by
others. We feel that if people get to know us as we
really are then they may not like us and will then
reject what they see. This is why we cover up by

imitating other people, by taking on some behavioural pattern which we admire in someone else. It is amazing the lengths to which we will go in order to hide our true selves. We forget that the precious and unique individual which lies beneath the layers of self-protection is bursting with potential, simply because that individual has been born again by the Spirit of God. I once heard someone say that our life is a hall of mirrors. We can either look at the reflection of ourselves that we see in the mirror of man's approval or the reflection we see in the mirror of God's truth. If we are looking in the mirror of man's approval then we will never truly be free to be ourselves because we will always be striving to perform in order to please someone else. The trouble with that is that our performance always falls short of what we are trying to achieve because we set our goals unrealistically high in order to gain the acceptance we so desperately need from others. The consequence of that is a feeling of guilt because we do not match up to what we think we ought to be. Think of all the wasted energy in that process!

But if we look in the mirror of God's truth, then we are reminded that we are his creation, that we are unique. The picture is then very different. Ephesians 2:10 talks of us being God's workmanship. In Greek this word means 'masterpiece'. What a wonderful thought that is, that when God looks at you and me, he is looking at his masterpiece. Because of Christ, he accepts me totally as I am. There is no need to strive to perform in order to win God's approval because we have Christ. Therefore by faith we dare to be ourselves before him and before others. The mirror of God's truth – his word – liberates us to be the people he intended us to be. This should give us tremendous confidence. *We can never be more loved by God than we are now.* No matter how long we may live there is nothing we can ever do that will make God love us any more than he does today. Therefore we can relax and concentrate with him on developing those many facets that go to make up the real person inside.

Getting to know yourself can be a very exciting experience. Like getting to know anyone else, we have to begin by asking questions of ourselves. What am I interested in? What do I feel strongly about? What are the things that move me deeply or the things that make me laugh? What are the things that make me angry or sad? What am I afraid of and why? Am I hiding behind some imitation of someone else? Why have I chosen that person to imitate? What do I admire about them and why do I want to be like them? What is it that I feel I lack? How can I talk to God about that and sort it out with him?

By asking questions prayerfully of ourselves and of God, we will gradually get to know the person inside. Who knows, we may even get to like what we see!

I will never forget a colleague telling me about a member of staff who had just joined the company. She asked me if I had seen him. When I replied that I hadn't, and asked her what he looked like, she said, quite seriously, 'Well . . . he looks like a Christian – you know – dull.' God forbid that we should be hideous caricatures of what he designed us to be! Can you thank God for *you*? Can you thank him for what you're going to become by his grace – a God-made individual in your own right? A few months prior to my writing this, I heard of the death of a lady whom I had the privilege of knowing quite well. She was severely disabled and only partially sighted. It was a major effort for her to get to church each week, even though she was taken there by friends. She could do little for herself and was heavily dependent on help from others. But she was a wonderful character – a true individual. She was witty, compassionate, loving, delightful to know. She spent many hours a day praying for others, reading the Bible *and* newspapers (!), helping younger Christians to develop their own relationship with God. It was a pleasure and a challenge to be in her company *because she was herself*.

We are all tempted to fall into the error of judging the value of people by what they achieve, how they stand in public opinion, what they have written or what they say. The classic Old Testament example is that of Samuel, sent to choose one of Jesse's sons to be king of Israel (1 Samuel 16:4–13). As each handsome young man stepped before Samuel it seemed obvious that there was monarch material in all of them. But God spoke: 'The LORD does not look at the things man looks at. Man looks at the outward appearance, but the LORD looks at the heart' (verse 7).

The Lord values us, not for what we have done, nor for what others think of us, but because we are how we are, the one he made, and valued highly enough to die for.

# CHAPTER SIX

# Hold your Head High

As we begin to appreciate our potential in Christ we will also begin to communicate it. It is a fact that we are communicating all the time. Whether good or bad, the communication never ceases. Non-verbal communication means the way we communicate outside the things we say and how we say them. It embraces our mannerisms, actions and life-style. Non-verbal communication is important because it is not wholly dependent on our speech. In a group we are communicating to anyone who might look at us, although we may or may not be aware of it. I have often wondered what I communicate to people who can't hear what I am saying in a group context, but who can see me, my mannerisms and actions, my facial expressions, my posture.

In the last chapter we looked briefly at some verses in 1 Peter 2. We saw there that what we have become in Christ by faith is a 'chosen people, a royal priesthood, a holy nation'. That means that each one of us individually has become a Very Important Person. Of course, our importance has nothing to do with our own merit or our own achievements. It is based purely on our position in Jesus Christ and what he has done for us. But nevertheless, we *are* part of a royal family.

Part of a chosen race. As we think, therefore, about the way we communicate, it is vital that we remember what we are, what we have become.

If we are unique – and we are – then we should be radiating that uniqueness. The Christian has every reason to hold his head high. He is forgiven of his sins, he has been born again; he belongs to the King of Kings. God the Creator and Lord of all has become his father.

I am always saddened by the number of Christians who hang their heads down, figuratively and literally. So many of us communicate an apologetic attitude, a lack of confidence about who we are. A colleague of mine temporarily rejected Christianity because the only Christians she had met were dull and apologetic. Her words were, 'No umph!'

## A daughter of the King of Kings

Before I became a Christian I had very poor posture. I am tall and like many tall people I have the problem of slouching, of not standing up straight. But part of the reason for my posture being so bad was that I didn't want to stand out above other people. I was taller than most of my friends and I didn't want to be different. The thought of being different made me insecure and shy and I didn't want anything about me to make me conspicuous. Consequently I tried to adjust my height by hanging my head down! My clothes, too, reflected the same kind of protective mechanism that I was employing in my posture. I wore drab colours, uninteresting clothes. I didn't want to be noticed. I wanted to blend in with the background.

After I became a Christian, I was talking with

someone whom I had only seen on two or three previous occasions. We certainly didn't know each other very well. During the short conversation we had she said, 'Val, do you mind if I say something rather personal?'

I didn't dare say I did mind so I hesitantly said, 'No, I don't mind. Go ahead.'

She asked me, 'Do you believe that you are born again?'

'Yes, of course,' I answered.

She said, 'Do you then believe that you are a daughter of the King of Kings?'

I said, 'Yes, I do.'

'Then, in that case,' she went on, 'you believe that you are a member of God's royal family?'

And I said, 'Yes, I suppose I do believe that.'

She said, 'May I say then with every respect that you don't carry yourself as though you are.'

It was a shock to hear somebody say something like that to me. I was hurt, but what she said did make me think. Later on, I began to realize that my self-image left a lot to be desired. I hadn't really grasped the truth of who I was in Jesus Christ and the importance of my life to him. So important that he was prepared to give his life in place of mine. The more I meditated on what Jesus had done for me and how much he loved me, the more I realized how right my friend had been. In hanging my head down and wearing drab clothes and looking insignificant, I was actually denying a wonderful thing, a miracle that had happened in my life. I decided there and then to do something about it. I told the same friend to prod me in the back every time she saw me slouch. She promised she would and she was very faithful! I then went to another friend who had good dress sense and asked if she would go shopping with me. I needed to buy some new clothes.

I had always believed that God has made us stewards of everything that he has given to us in this life but that was the first time I ever realized that being a good steward of the person God had made me was going to involve spending some money, and it was a new thought to me. It was hard to see myself in smarter clothes. In brighter colours. It was even harder to combine that with standing up straight and holding my head up. It was a constant daily battle but I asked God to help me and he did. By faith, I began to learn to communicate *what I was*: the Very Important Person I had become!

I am not talking about fashion here. I am not recommending one particular fashion trend above another for either men or women. What I am saying is that it is very easy for us to use our clothes and our posture to hide, to protect ourselves from stepping out and communicating that uniqueness and the knowledge of it which gives us the confidence and 'presence', that 'something' which is never seen in the life of an unbeliever.

Some years ago a man I knew quite well was at a conference where these things were being discussed. A great deal of emphasis was placed on our position in Christ, what he had done for us, and what we have become by trusting him as our Saviour. The person in question had always considered himself to be very plain and uninteresting, not only in his looks but also in his personality and character. He didn't feel he had much to offer in any of those aspects of his life. But at that conference God got through to him. He suddenly realized, for the first time, what Jesus had done on the cross for him. He realized how much he was loved. He realized how important he must have been to God for Jesus to do that, and to make that incalculable sacrifice for him. He realized too that he was forgiven totally and that by faith and through God's grace he was now raised to the heavenly places in Christ.

The change in that young man was remarkable. His facial expressions changed. He began to smile. His whole bearing changed. His posture changed. He began to stand up straight. He began to look more relaxed. In his relationships he became more outgoing and dared to take the initiative. He became more concerned with the other person than with himself and how he was coming across. As time went on, he began to pay attention to his clothes and his hair. I believe that this tremendous change was largely due to his new realization of his position in Christ.

## How do you sit?

We are unique. We are members of God's royal family, and we need to acknowledge that in our bearing, our attitude and so on. Have you ever paid attention to how you sit down? That may seem a very strange question, but we do spend a great percentage of our lives sitting down. The way we do it can communicate an awful lot.

How do you sit down? I know many people who always sit on the edge of their chair, bolt upright with their hands folded on their lap and their feet together. I am never comfortable with people who are sitting in a position like that. I feel uncomfortable on their behalf and I begin to wonder what they are thinking. Perhaps they feel threatened or maybe they're wondering what's going to come out of the conversation. They just *look* ill at ease!

By sitting back in a chair and relaxing we are communicating that we want to be there, that we want to be with the other person. It's up to you and me to take the initiative. Decide to take the responsibility. It is up to us to communicate, 'I want to be with you. I want you to be with me.' It should be our objective to put the other person at ease. We will not do this if we are sitting bolt upright, looking like something you throw things at in a fairground!

There is something which has helped me over the years, particularly in a difficult situation, if I'm meeting people for the first time or if I'm feeling generally ill at ease. When I sit down, I sit well back in the chair and take four seconds. One: is my back comfortable in the chair? Two: what am I going to do with my legs? Am I going to cross them? Three: are my shoulders down and relaxed? This will determine what I will do with my arms. And four: is my head comfortable or is it perched stiffly on top of my shoulders, like a skittle? By taking these four seconds, you can ensure that no matter what you *feel*, you will communicate a relaxed posture. If my objective is to serve the other person and radiate God's love then I can trust God to enable me to do that. I may not often feel relaxed or feel that I want to take the initiative, but that's where my faith must come in: to do what I know to be right, not what I feel I should do.

## How do you shake hands?

How do you respond when you are introduced to someone for the first time? There are many ways of greeting someone on initial introduction and shaking hands is one of them. In my line of business, men and women alike shake hands quite often. This form of greeting can, however, be either a very pleasant experience or a remarkably revolting one!

It never ceases to amaze me how many people offer a piece of wet fish to squeeze when they offer you their hand! I'm sure all of us have at some time in our lives had the wet fish handshake. Perhaps you cannot help having moist hands, but you can help how you grip the other person's. A half-hearted handshake communicates to me a half-hearted greeting.

If we are seeking to serve the other person, to put them at their ease, to be concerned with how they're feeling, then surely we should offer a firm, friendly handshake. It's a gesture which says, 'I am glad to know you and I hope you are glad to know me.'

I can think of several people I know who, when they shake your hand, make you feel that you are the most important person in the world at the moment. Even before they have said anything, their facial expression welcomes you, they look you in the eye, they take your hand and grasp it firmly. You feel that they are genuinely pleased to see you. What a difference between that and an experience I had some years ago.

I was introduced to a very mature Christian who had known the Lord for many years. But when I shook hands with him, he didn't look me in the eye and he put his head down. He offered me a piece of wet fish to squeeze instead of a firm handshake and muttered something about, 'How do you do?' I didn't know anyone at that particular function and I was feeling very lonely. He had been there many times and if he had wanted to, he could have made me feel more comfortable. As it was, he only made me feel more isolated and lonely.

I couldn't help but wonder, if I had been an unbeliever, what sort of impression I would have had about Christians? If we truly believe that we are a chosen people, a royal priesthood, a holy nation, then we are going to communicate that. We are going to have a presence. It will make us attractive, approachable and more effective as we reach out to unbelievers.

## Do you scare people?

What about those people who are naturally out-going, and who have no difficulty in communicating with others? It is worth checking with God if that confidence you have is really consecrated. I have known Christians who have communicated an arrogance and an over-confident attitude which not only is dishonouring to God but certainly does not communicate the kind of life that we are discussing in this book. An arrogant Christian will frighten the shy and retiring, and irritate those who are more confident. Knowing what Christ has done for us through his death should humble us as nothing else can. Whereas it is true that we can confidently hold our heads high, that confidence must be contained in quiet humility – a humble confidence. A strength with gentleness. This is something we can pray for and I believe that God will answer our prayers. Certainly if we are growing in Christian character, then those qualities which we associate with the new nature should filter through to our outward communication. But, in truth, this does not always happen automatically. Therefore we need to look carefully at our outward communication, what we project by how we are.

Because of my old problems of posture and holding my head down, I pray often about my bearing, my countenance, the expression in my eyes. We are taught in Scripture, 'You do not have, because you do not ask God' (James 4:2), so why not ask God specifically for our non-verbal communication to reflect Jesus and to be positively attractive?

# What about life-style?

Much of what we communicate about ourselves is found in our life-style, and this is nearly always a sensitive issue. Life-style is a very individual thing, and each of us has to decide before God what is right for us.

We should prayerfully consider the kind of ministry we are involved in, or perhaps the kind of neighbourhood we live in. The kind of work we do or the kind of people we are wanting to reach. Of course it also depends on our finances. Whether we are married or not. What we feel we can justify spending our money on. But we do communicate through our life-style, through our home and what it looks like. The kind of car we drive (or bicycle we ride!). The kind of furniture we have. The way we decorate our homes. This is all part of the communication of ourselves. It is an extension of our personality.

There is one particular home in which I always feel relaxed. Not a lot of money has been spent on it. The furnishings are quite simple and inexpensive but thought has gone into the way the room is laid out and the use of lighting. Walking into the room you feel welcome because it offers a very relaxed atmosphere. You want to be there, you come to rest. It reflects the people who live in the house. Their personalities show through in the kind of ornaments, the kind of books, the kind of plants and furniture they have in their home.

It's quite obvious to me that the owners of that house have taken the responsibility to ensure that people who come to their home are put at their ease. They have taken the initiative in helping visitors to feel relaxed. And it certainly works.

Many Christians in the world today live by the philosophy 'cheapest is best'. The cheaper the better, and if you can get it for nothing, that's wonderful. Please don't misunderstand me here. I am in no way referring to people who cannot afford to buy the things that they would like to have. That is a different matter altogether. I am referring to those Christians who by choice have decided to live a very primitive and spartan existence. This can be something they feel God has asked them to do and I realize that I am touching on a very sensitive issue. I do know people who feel very strongly that they should live a very simple life-style. They have prayed carefully and thoroughly about it and they feel before God that it should be so. But the key for them lies in the fact that they have prayed carefully and thoroughly. I have also spoken to Christians who feel that simply because they are Christians, they should have a very spartan home. Some even refuse to buy anything new. It is not that a simple life-style is wrong, but that it is wrong if we choose it for the wrong reasons. Because we believe it is the 'Christian' thing to do. It is very right if it is a conviction that God has given us.

There is no such thing as a 'Christian' life-style. Scripture does teach us temperance in all things and that is a good guideline. If we are praying regularly that God will keep us from the temptations a materialistic society presents all the time, then I believe he will be faithful to guide us in how we spend our money and in the kind of life we lead. In all these things, it is only through faith that we can please God. We follow God's lead either to live a simple, spartan life or to spend money on doing things to our home because God will use that home to minister to others.

I know one family who have a very attractive home. Their main ministry outside their work is holding small dinner parties for unbelieving friends. The people concerned seem to be very gifted in entertaining. They know how to make someone feel relaxed and at home, and guests soon feel as though they are part of the family.

The house is not very large and they found that the small rooms limited the number of people they could have at one time to their dinner parties. They prayed long and hard about it. God gave them the means to have two small rooms knocked into one in order to accommodate more people. This is a very expensive alteration to have done, but these people felt that it was good stewardship of what God had given. Looking at the whole of the situation in context, looking at the gifts that God had given them and the way he uses them with other people, it became clear that their effectiveness could increase if they had more space.

This is another example of spending money in order to be a good steward of something God has given us. The context of the situation is important. In another context a decision like that could have been totally inappropriate.

As I mentioned before, our life-style is often determined by the kind of people we are mixing with, the kind of neighbourhood we live in. We must be sensitive to the people we are likely to have in our homes. We need to be aware of the kind of atmosphere that would make them feel comfortable. Remember, we take the responsibility for putting them at their ease. Taking factors like them into consideration helps us as we're deciding how to plan specifically the home we should have and the life-style we should adopt.

## What should I wear?

Just as there is no such thing as a Christian life-style, there is also no such thing as the 'Christian' wardrobe. Have you ever been tempted to ask yourself, 'Is this the kind of thing a Christian should wear?' Or, 'The other Christians at my church don't wear things like this – maybe I shouldn't either.' Many Christians today are afraid to look striking or fashionable or even just plain smart! They feel it would be out of place for a Christian to look that way. I don't know where that idea comes from but I can only think that there was some misunderstanding generations ago which has taken root and been passed down through the ages. Even Jesus himself had a very expensive and very beautiful cloak. It was so beautiful that the soldiers cast lots for it after his crucifixion, rather than dividing it between them.

Scripture is very clear on many things. It leaves us in no doubt about certain things which it lays down clearly as sins. But there are many areas about which there is no specific guidance. It would appear that often they are neither right nor wrong. What matters is the spirit in which they are done. I am not suggesting by all this that the Christian should be immodest or sexually tempting through the clothes he or she wears. Certainly Scripture teaches us to exercise modesty and not dress seductively. I am conscious that some, especially recently committed Christians, need the opposite advice – to dress less seductively.

What I am saying is that what we choose to wear is something which we decide before God. As long as we are not causing someone to sin or stumble, then we are at total liberty to wear what we choose. Let me add hastily, after saying that we should not cause others to stumble, that I do not mean don't cause others irritation because

they feel we should be wearing something else! –
as sometimes happens in Christian groups and
churches. If someone else does not like the clothes
I wear then that is not my problem, it is theirs.

We should carry ourselves and dress ourselves
as the children of the King of Kings. We dress first
and foremost for our Heavenly Father, and so, like
anything else we do for him, we should be talking
to him about it first. Let us please keep away from
the 'Christian Wardrobe'!

## 'Christian' novelties

Moving away from clothes now, what do you
think about Jesus stickers and Jesus calendars? I
have (from time to time) had calendars in my home
with verses of Scripture printed on them. There
are, in fact, some very well-designed and attractive
calendars and other Christian printed goods on
the market – car stickers, badges, 'One Way'
stickers, T-shirts, sweat shirts and so on. Lots of
ways to communicate scriptural truths in a fun
way.

I am not suggesting that these novelties are
wrong, but I would like to toss out a challenge. If
we use them, do we use them simply because they
are there and because a lot of other Christians use
them? Do we use them perhaps as an easy way of
witnessing? Or do we use them because we have
prayed through our non-verbal communication
and we feel before God very strongly that we
should use this kind of tool to back up our general
witness?

When used prayerfully they can be very powerful. A friend of mine places a new verse of

Scripture above her desk each month on a very large piece of paper. Some of her colleagues have cringed in discomfort at the sight of it! And yet one evening as the security guard was checking around the building, he saw the verse above the desk and as a result became a Christian.

Tools like these are not wrong in themselves. I am only suggesting that we check whether we have really asked God about their use. Is this what he is wanting us to do at this time and in this place? Or are we just taking it for granted that this is acceptable Christian behaviour? If we are doing that, then we may find that it has just the opposite effect. It might put people off rather than bring them closer to knowing God.

Scripture verses can be and certainly are used, just as in my friend's office, to bring people to Christ. If a person is prepared and the verse of Scripture is appropriate, then they can at that same moment see their need of Christ and commit their lives to him. But it is worth saying that in the 1980s most people need time and help to become prepared to understand what a Bible verse can mean. Because their frame of reference is very different from ours and, indeed, from that of the non-Christian twenty years ago, they will, rather than accept the verse (or even ignore it), reject it. And so we need to be prayerful in how we use calendars, verses, badges, Jesus stickers.

# What do people see in us?

I was very pleased to hear a comment being made one day about a colleague who is a Christian. The person concerned had just been giving a talk to new people joining the company. She had been speaking for only forty minutes and had never met that group before. Afterwards, apparently, one of the newcomers said to another, 'I really enjoyed that lady's presentation the best. She seemed to have got it all together. She looked as though she knew where she was going. A whole person. I really enjoyed her.'

That is a very fine testimony to have. Someone else once said about that same person, 'If ever I do get round to seriously considering Christianity for myself, it's that lady I want to talk to. You just feel she knows not only what the world's about but what God's about too.'

To sum up then, our non-verbal, often unconscious, communication is very important and demands our prayerful attention. How we greet people, hold ourselves, sit, dress, furnish our houses or rooms . . . What do people see in us? And that is a double-edged question. They probably see in us what our outward self tells them. So our non-verbal communication matters.

Yet, as the last illustration shows, more important than the outward appearance is the quiet confidence of inner security. 'She looked as though she knew where she was going. A whole person . . .' You can't look like that if you are not a whole person. Part of being whole is to be comfortable in the presence of our own emotions. So read on.

# Your Emotions Matter

Emotion is a very difficult thing to define. Certainly it has to do with feelings, with our reactions and responses to certain stimuli and situations. These things can affect our behaviour either positively or adversely. We can have positive emotions that make us happy. We can have unpleasant emotions that make us sad or angry. Other times we just 'feel' emotion and can't define it.

Often we feel that emotion gets in the way of what we want to achieve. We think of our feelings as a nuisance. Consequently many people suppress their emotions and sometimes ignore them altogether. Other people 'wear their heart on their sleeve' to the point that their emotions get the better of them.

Perhaps we could loosely define emotion as being that dimension of our lives which enables us to *experience* something as opposed to merely receiving information mentally. It is a tremendously important dimension and if it is not consecrated and brought within the control of Christ, then we can become its slave. However, if, through Christ, we become its master, then emotion enriches and enhances all aspects of life. Things take on new colour when our appreciation of them includes the way we feel.

So we are talking in this chapter about that dimension of life which enables us to feel and to experience. There is a beautiful passage of Scripture in the book of Hosea. There, perhaps more than anywhere else in the Bible, we see clearly that God has an emotional side to his character. Chapter 11 is a very moving account of God's emotional reaction to Israel's turning away from him. But in verse 8 God says, 'How can I hand you over, Israel? . . . My heart is changed within me; all my compassion is aroused.'

God the Father obviously has very deep and compassionate feelings. It therefore follows that his creation – mankind – should also be blessed with the ability and the facility to feel very deeply. Just as it is an integral part of God's character, so it is intended to be an integral part of ours. Without it we would be cold, and would resemble walking robots rather than created human beings.

Someone once said to me that he felt he was 'sitting on an emotional volcano'. He could sense that buried beneath layers of self-protection was a lot of emotion that had never been tapped, never even been looked at. This is a very common phenomenon, especially among the British! Many of us are afraid of what lies lurking beneath the surface and because emotion is so potentially volatile, we would rather leave well alone than go rooting to see what is really there. On the surface we appear calm and in control and yet underneath there may be a seething mass of emotion which has never been recognized or dealt with.

If that is the case then a very large part of the person that God has made is locked away. When I was a very new Christian I was talking to a friend who told me about Christian love and how she was learning to demonstrate this. She said to me, 'I am learning how I can love people without using my emotions. I've decided that it is possible and in fact necessary to prevent me from getting hurt. I am going to keep my emotions locked away. I don't want to know what is there. My love for people is going to be purely and simply practical.'

Even though I was a new Christian, this somehow didn't ring true to me. I couldn't help thinking that there was something very wrong in a kind of love which was purely practical and had no emotional content at all. I began to ask myself, 'But what about things like compassion and understanding? Surely those are all part of emotion too and part of love? So how can anyone love coldly and practically without any kind of emotion at all?' Needless to say my friend ran into difficulties and eventually had to face the fact that her emotions needed to be accepted, recognized and brought before God for his control over them, that they couldn't just be sat on and suppressed.

# Fear of emotion

Trying to live life as a Christian without including the emotional dimension of that life is really to deny part of the nature of God which is dwelling within us. Scripture teaches us that we gradually take on the very nature of God, as we live with him. So how can we ever be real people, able to relate to other people, able to understand other people, able to influence other people, if one of the most dynamic facets of that nature is missing?

It is interesting to observe how many people are afraid of this thing called emotion. Certainly many Christians see emotion as a threat to their disciplined life with God and so they push what they feel to one side. They are afraid that what they feel might not only displease God, but might stand in the way of some objective decision that needs to be made, or some task that must be completed. Other Christians believe that their emotions should be expressed freely and feel that the disciplined kind of walk with God is a stifling one and smacks of legalism.

Both groups are right to a certain extent. Somewhere between the two, there is a balance. Emotion was not given to us to be a threat to our life with God, but like any other dimension in our lives it was given as yet another channel through which we glorify the God who made us. Therefore it is important that we prayerfully, and on the basis of Scripture, look at this potentially dynamic aspect of our humanity and learn how to demonstrate effective stewardship of it.

This surely begins by recognizing the existence of emotion in our make-up. Whether we are aware of it or not, it is there. Then we can learn to identify specific feelings in order to have God deal with them. First of all, let's look at those people who have difficulty in expressing emotion. Usually, their lives are controlled. They would rather not feel things, but simply get on and do them. They have aims that they quite rightly want to achieve and they will not allow emotion to get in the way of achieving them.

Some years ago, I knew someone who admitted that she was this kind of person. She was capable, gifted and very disciplined. But somewhere along the line she began to sense that the emotional dimension of her life was undeveloped. She began to pray about it. She asked God to show her what she was actually feeling about things. She had become so used to pushing aside her emotions that often she would go through a day quite mechanically. After she had been praying about this for some time, things began to happen. Her job became very difficult. She had a very irritating colleague. She developed a relationship with someone which triggered off pent-up emotion that she had never experienced before. Her responsibilities in the church began to weigh heavily on her. There were difficulties, frustrations. People were making demands on her.

Suddenly, this life which had been up to now so very controlled was bombarded with people and circumstances which touched some emotion in her life. She felt attacked from all sides and didn't know what to do. She probably wished that she had never asked God to help her in the first place! For the first time in her life she felt personally attacked by a colleague and so she felt hurt. This was new to her. She felt frustrated through the situation at church. Suddenly it was out of her control. She felt anger at injustice that she saw in her job. It was as though someone had pulled a rug from under her feet and she lost her balance.

But in allowing that to happen, God could then start rebuilding. Slowly but surely she began to take each emotion that she experienced to God. She took the hurt she felt and asked him to deal with it. She took the anger to God and asked forgiveness. She took the frustration to God and asked him to cleanse her from wanting things her way and to teach her patience.

Bit by bit, as God brought the various emotions to the surface, she scooped them off and surrendered them to God. In time she was able to distinguish between good and bad feelings, between those that God gave her to enjoy and to enrich her life and those which were potentially destructive and needed to be recognized as sin and taken to the cross for forgiveness. Needless to say the change in her was quite remarkable. She became understanding, compassionate, caring. She became more thoughtful and more concerned about others and less concerned about achieving the aims that she had set for herself. She even changed in appearance. She became more gentle and much more approachable. She became a real person. Evidence of emotion had once been considered by her to be weak. Now she was learning about the strength that comes when it is surrendered to the power and control of God.

There is nothing weak about emotion. As my friend learned, some of the most attractive men and women are those who show living, and yet controlled, emotion in their lives. Their experience of life is very obvious and yet it is an experience which is very obviously under the control of Christ. Controlled, yet not suppressed, it is a very beautiful and attractive reflection of God in their lives.

## Scripture the key

We are afraid of emotion because of its unpredictability, its power and its indefinable shape. It is a nebulous mass. It is intangible. So the tangible must be applied to give it shape. This is exactly what Scripture does. It gives shape to the feelings we cannot define. Bringing our innermost feelings, however vague, under the spotlight of scriptural truth is one of the most effective ways of learning to control them.

God is fully aware of how we feel. In Psalm 38:9 David says, 'All my longings lie open before you, O Lord; my sighing is not hidden from you'. Nothing we feel goes unseen by God. He is there in it with us and that is such a comforting thought when feelings are difficult to identify. We can take them to God as they are, in their shapeless form, and remind him that he knows about them anyway. Then, we have the confidence that as we begin to apply Scripture to these things, God will be there to give them the shape that we can identify and deal with.

We need to go back to the absolutes of the word, the unchanging truths of Scripture, and to apply the appropriate truth to whatever emotion we are feeling. I cannot emphasize too much our need of Scripture. A specific time, set aside each day for reading and meditating upon God's word, is vital to our spiritual survival. Only then will we find the precious truths available to us.

I am one of those people who wear their heart on their sleeve. My emotions are very near the surface. I feel things very deeply and it shows! Some years ago, this was a real problem to me. Someone once said that I was 'emotionally unstable'. I suppose this was true. I could be thrown very easily by circumstances or by a comment from someone. I could be very tearful. I could be very angry. My responses were governed solely by what I was feeling at the time. This meant that my behaviour was generally erratic and not very reliable, and there was an instability which was damaging my relationship with God and other people. Then I remembered a verse which someone had shared with me in Proverbs: 'The Lord tears down the house of the proud, but he will make secure the boundaries of the [consecrated] widow' (15:25, Amplified). I had previously learned this verse in Dutch during my time in Holland. In Dutch the verse talks about *grenspalen*. These are stakes which support a boundary fence. I could see the wisdom of this analogy. Each one of those stakes represented a truth of Scripture that was appropriate to whatever need I might have emotionally. I started to look at some of these truths. I have mentioned some in a previous chapter. I am forgiven. I am accepted in the Beloved. God wants the best for my life. He is a righteous God.

During that time I was in the process of changing my job and was having considerable difficulty in finding just the right one. I had become extremely discouraged and very low. My emotional state was perhaps worse than it had ever been. I was as low as I could get without totally breaking up. I applied for many positions, and almost as many turned me down. I reached the point where I dreaded receiving each day's mail.

Out of all the jobs I had applied for, there was one which above all the rest I dearly wanted. It sounded just the right thing. I had built my hopes on this one particular job and I knew that I would be terribly disappointed if I was refused. However, I was also very slowly, but surely, learning some of the lessons God was teaching me about not being so dependent on feelings.

I remember one day very clearly when the postman came and a letter fell on the mat. It was from the company that I had applied to for the job I wanted so much. I picked up the envelope and looked at it. Suddenly, God reminded me that I was not dependent on my feelings. That my behaviour and my life no longer needed to be in the grip of what I felt. His words were true and I needed to grasp that truth. Before I opened the envelope, I prayed and I said to God, 'Lord, I don't know what is going to be in this letter, and at this moment I don't feel that you love me. I feel almost as though you're not even there. But despite what I feel, I am going to hold on to the truth that you do want the best of my life because you love me. The Bible is truth, therefore at this moment I am choosing to believe what I know to be true and not what I feel.' I then added in my prayer, 'Whatever I find in this letter I will take as being your perfect will for my life at this moment.'

I opened it and the answer was a clear refusal, but the peace I experienced, even in my disappointment, was tremendous! The lesson for me there was that, before I knew what was going to happen I had chosen to trust God because of the truth of his word. I could not have been much lower that day but God met me in my need. It was just one in a series of lessons from God to build into my life an emotional stability. The truth that I had chosen to use that day – that God wants the best for my life – was, you could say, the first stake being hammered into the ground. Others followed.

When my feelings told me that God could not forgive me a certain thing, I would take the truth that 'God is faithful and just and will forgive us our sins and purify us from all unrighteousness' (1 John 1:9). That was another stake hammered into the ground and so it went on and still does go on, until a series of stakes firmly rooted in the ground surround me. Between those stakes hangs a fence of God's love and grace and protection and within that fence I am safe. This does not mean that I am emotionally strong. What it does mean is that God's strength and power are gradually being made perfect in my existing weakness. If God should take his hand away from me I would be exactly where I was before. But holding on to the word of God, reading, learning by heart, thinking carefully about its truths, has helped me build a healthy structure in my life.

## Identify the leaks and know how to plug them

It can be an exciting experience, choosing the right truth for each need. There will always be a truth for whatever need we may have, and learning to identify our emotions is a very liberating thing. It can mean that we are liberating ourselves from unconscious sin, or lack of faith. How often have you felt generally miserable about a situation? You feel depressed about it. You feel down, maybe frustrated, unhappy. You can't seem to put your finger on what is wrong. Should anyone ask, 'How do you feel?', you would probably say something like, 'Oh, just generally out of sorts. I feel down, I feel miserable.' Sometimes, of course, the reason is simply that we *are* just out of sorts. But often it is the result of something that has happened, some circumstances in our lives, or something for which we are not fully trusting God. Whatever we may be feeling, whatever has happened, we must go to God and ask him to untangle the web of emotion that we might be feeling at that moment, and show us very clearly if there is any sin in our lives, or anything in which we're not trusting him.

In her book, *Lord of My Rocking Boat*, Carole Mayhall addresses this issue of lack of trust in areas of our lives. She talks of 'waves' of crisis which enter our lives suddenly and without warning, and her book gives suggestions as to how to deal with these. But as well as the large waves which suddenly rush into the boat of our lives, there are also 'leaks', perhaps hidden areas of our lives in which we are not fully trusting God.

It wasn't so much the water splashing over the sides which was causing me pain but the water coming in through the cracks. Water can seep in through cracks even on a quiet sea. In Mark, Chapter 4, it was a great storm which first challenged me about the angry waves in my life, but even in calm waters my boat will sink if it has a lot of internal ruptures. Water either buoys us up or drowns us, depending on what shape our boat is in, so the answer to the little waves

and leaks is my internal maintenance.
(*Lord of My Rocking Boat*: Carole Mayhall (NAV-PRESS, 1981))

God will, if we ask him, reveal these 'leaks' to us. We can then acknowledge them for what they are, sin and lack of faith. They are then no longer a shapeless mass of mixed emotion. They have become concrete and we can deal with them.

Jesus did not come to die for mixed-up emotions, but for sin. I believe that often when we are feeling mixed up or overwhelmed by something, it's because deep down there is sin lurking somewhere under those feelings.

Someone I knew years ago once told me that her home life was very difficult. She was very unhappy because of her relationship with her father. He was domineering and made many demands on her. As time went on, she became more and more upset. She felt that her love for him was being spurned. She tried everything to win his affection. Finally she became extremely depressed and emotionally unable to cope any more. When she told her friends about it, she felt guilty and disloyal to her father. But in time, she began to realize that there was something underneath that was causing her far more pain than the actual situation with her father. She realized that she disliked him intensely and hadn't been able to face that fact. When she finally did, and confessed it as sin, she experienced a tremendous release and relief.

It is Satan's objective always to keep us away from God. Clouding our mind to sin is one of the ways he will do it. In this case he did it by bringing before my friend's eyes her responsibility of loyalty to her father. To admit even to herself that she disliked him so much would have made her feel very disloyal. Because of that she couldn't bear to face the fact that she felt so violently towards him. But in facing it, and confessing it, she was forgiven.

We really do need to be aware of how Satan will use our emotions to keep us from the cleansing power of the cross. It is quite understandable that he will use our feelings, because of their intangible nature. We can become entangled in them as in a spider's web, not knowing which way to go on. Not knowing the way out. But God is in there with us and he promises victory as we obey him.

As we do this we are freed to enjoy those things he gave us to enhance our lives. We are able to love without fear. We can drink in the warmth of a summer day and thank God for the thrill it gives us. We can allow ourselves to be deeply moved by some piece of music and know that it is God who has given us that ability to appreciate such a creation. We can laugh, we can sympathize; we can weep, we can sing for joy. Rather than suppressing what we feel, obedience to the word of God liberates us to be 'feeling people'.

# Words Work for You

They had been seated at the table for around fifteen minutes. Most of them were well into their first course. Janet looked round the table. No-one said a word. Everyone was diligently tucking into their own food without paying much attention to anyone else. Up to this point, not one word had been spoken since the meal began. Had Janet not taken the initiative to ask some simple questions, the meal would most probably have continued in complete silence.

This was a Christian conference. Delegates had come from all over Britain to hear the word of God and to have fellowship. Janet thought: 'This is going to be a wonderful weekend!' This may be an extreme example, but perhaps we should ask ourselves, 'How well do we communicate verbally?' If we are a 'chosen race and a royal priesthood' then surely we should be able to talk!

People sometimes say, 'I am not very good at talking and holding conversations with people. I would rather just sit and listen.' Many of us feel that way from time to time but the facility we have to communicate with words is a very wonderful gift. If you stop and think for a moment of the sophistication of that faculty which we call speech, then surely we must marvel at the wisdom and creativity of our Creator God. Speech is not just a set of words strung together in sentences. Words can change their meaning by the intonation of the voice or the emphasis we place upon them. The sounds we make in our speech communicate so much of what we are inside and what we're feeling at that moment. It's a gift which we should try to develop in order to glorify God.

You may have heard the old saying, 'Your actions speak so loudly I can't hear what you're saying'. Well, that works the other way round too. If our non-verbal communication is strong and positive we can spoil everything as soon as we open our mouths! Speech, inflection and intonation can encourage, can communicate love and care, but they can also damage and hurt. We need to ensure that our speech is controlled by God and is working for us in communicating that we are indeed God's family.

Colossians 4:6 says, 'Let your conversation be always full of grace, seasoned with salt, so that you may know how you ought to answer everyone.' What is 'gracious' speech? The Oxford Dictionary defines it as 'agreeable, pleasing, kindly, benevolent, courteous'. If we glance back to those verses in 1 Peter 2 about our being a chosen people, a royal priesthood and so on, then it follows that not only should our attitude reflect the position we have in Christ – that humble confidence we talked about – but so should our speech. Gracious speech is positive speech. 'Agreeable, pleasing, kindly, courteous' – these are all positive attitudes. This doesn't mean that Christians should be sweet and sugary. There are few things more irritating than a sugary, over-sweet Christian! But it does mean that as we endeavour to project a positive attitude in the way we talk, we serve others more effectively.

Many Christians communicate an apologetic attitude in their manner, and do the same in their speech. Have you ever talked to someone like this? Someone who is constantly apologizing or putting themselves in a negative light when telling you something? Many years ago, someone pointed out to me that in a short conversation, I had apologized in some form around ten times. I had been negative about myself. I had apologized when something fell on the floor (when in fact it wasn't I who had dropped it), and so on. I was quite alarmed. I hadn't realized how negatively I came across. I learned later that much of it was the result of my poor self-image. But as I began to realize my position in Christ, I noticed that I wanted to reflect that in my speech, and in time my apologizing did lessen. Occasionally I still fall into the same trap if I feel particularly threatened or unsure of myself, but usually it happens if I am not spending sufficient time with the Lord and with his word.

To talk to someone who has an apologetic attitude in their speech immediately makes you feel ill at ease. You feel sorry for the person; you feel insecure on their behalf. For the unbeliever it is even more difficult to understand. I was shocked to discover that the root of my apologetic speech was selfishness. Because I was unsure of myself I would back off from making definite or positive statements. I was so concerned with protecting myself that I was forgetting all about the person I was talking to.

It is part of maturity, isn't it, to communicate a

strength of voice and a kindliness of tone which open up the communication channels and transmit the quality of life which comes from knowing Jesus Christ personally. Some years ago I had dinner with three Christian businessmen. I was the only woman in the group but I was very impressed by each of them. They were all very 'manly' men. I couldn't help but notice that these men were excellent examples of 'gracious speech'. They were totally at ease with me as a woman. Their manner was very relaxed and their speech was positive, kindly, pleasing and courteous. What they said and the way they said it reflected a certain strength coupled with a gentleness that was very attractive. They asked questions to keep the conversation going. We talked about many things, not all spiritual, and I came away that evening thinking how much I had enjoyed the stimulating and refreshing conversation.

## The problem of jargon

Perhaps one of the biggest problems we Christians face in our speech is our jargon and Christian terminology. It's very easy to pick up phrases from one another. We do it all the time. We do it even in the secular context too, depending on the kind of people we mix with. Christian jargon is totally foreign to the unbeliever and smacks of an 'in group' to which they do not belong. Even the word 'non-Christian' is one that I am currently trying not to use too often. We talk, too, quite freely about someone having 'shared' something with us. We allow things to slip out, such as, 'Oh, that's an answer to prayer' or, 'Praise the Lord that happened' and so on. These bits of jargon can be very irritating to others, particularly unbelievers. I am amazed how quickly people do notice that you have picked up either jargon or inflection from someone else.

I remember one day that someone from another company came to visit me at my office. When he arrived I was on the telephone and so he had to wait a few moments in the reception area. I finished my call and went down to meet him. I had never met him before and as I walked towards him and held out my hand, I said, 'Mr Watson, I'm sorry to have kept you waiting, do come this way.' As we stepped into the lift, he turned to me and said, 'You have either spent some time in the United States or you have worked for an American organization.' I was astounded. I said, 'I have never been to America but I did work for several years with an American organization. How ever did you know?' He said, 'There is just something in the inflection of your voice that I picked up straight away.' He must have had a particularly sharp ear to notice that in the few words that I said, particularly as I thought I still had quite a Yorkshire note in my speech! But it did make me realize how easily we can adopt other peoples' characteristics without knowing it.

# Salt

Part of the objective in allowing God to develop our verbal communication is to serve others. It is a verbal way of loving. We take the responsibility for making the other person feel comfortable in our presence. It is part of showing Christian love, to put the other person first. If we look back at the verse in Colossians 4:6 we see there that our speech is to be 'seasoned with salt' as well as gracious. Salt is something which gives bite, which brings out the flavour of something else. Because God has commanded us to develop our speech, that it be seasoned with salt, we can come to him with confidence and ask him to show us how we can do that.

A meal without any saltiness is a very bland meal. It is uninteresting. A week later and you will have forgotten what you ate during that meal. It is the same with speech. If speech has no bite, then it is bland and uninteresting and will not be remembered. Develop some bite, some dynamic in the way we talk and people will want to know us better. There will be something tasty about the things we say and the way we say them. The 'saltiness' comes from the confidence we can have by being knowledgeable in just one or two areas, or being up to date in current affairs, having some informed opinions or convictions about issues of the day. By this I do not mean that we become dogmatic or inflexible, but that we are able to communicate that we have thought about certain things and have opinions about them. We can talk about those opinions, and ask questions of other people: 'What do you think about such and such?' Developing our knowledge and being informed on current affairs gives us an inroad into discussions with other people.

I have known Christians who are totally unaware of some very serious economic or political issue currently in the news simply because they do not take the trouble to read a newspaper. I believe Christians should have opinions about what is going on in the world today. Unbelievers think a great deal about world affairs and how they are affected by them. How can we ever hope to influence the world we live in if we never learn to discuss the issues that face the human race each day? Or incidentally, how can we pray intelligently for our country or our world if we're not informed about what is happening in them?

The art of asking questions is something I wish all Christians would develop. People love to talk about themselves and if we have just a few questions to keep the conversation going, we can get to know someone quite well in a reasonably short time. But it never ceases to amaze me how many people just don't do it! I remember many situations which could have been so much more friendly if only people had asked a few questions. One painful example of this was the evening a colleague invited me to dinner. Throughout the whole evening, neither she nor her husband asked me one question, except to ascertain if I wanted more potatoes! I tried to keep the conversation moving but it was hard work, and by the time I got home I was exhausted!

We need never be afraid to ask questions, even about the things we don't understand. I remember once talking to a man who had spent many years in the Middle East and was obviously very knowledgeable on the culture and the political developments in that part of the world. I am not very knowledgeable about Middle East affairs and as we were talking I began to feel rather embarrassed at my lack of knowledge. I suppose I could have bluffed my way through but you know what can happen if you do that – you get caught out! I decided to be honest and ask some questions that would give me a basis on which I could understand the things he was telling me. Contrary to what I had expected, he was delighted to be able to give me a background picture and we had a very interesting conversation.

If our questions are put in a positive and unembarrassed way, then our attitude will spark a positive response. But if we communicate total ignorance of a subject, if we're ashamed of our ignorance and not only ashamed but insecure because we are ashamed, then having a conversation with us will be like trying to walk through molasses! If on the other hand we say, confidently, 'Could you just explain to me why it is that such and such . . .?' then we are simply communicating the fact that we lack knowledge in that particular area. It makes a world of difference to the person we are talking to. Questions can be just as salty as statements.

I had been in Holland one month and all of that time had been spent in language school. On leaving the school my command of the Dutch language extended just a little beyond the basic survival phrases! One evening I was at a party and was introduced to a young man who was delighted that I had 'learned his language' (that was a laugh for a start). He launched into a non-stop monologue, totally ignoring the fact that I was trying to tell him I didn't understand. After what seemed to me to be two years, he said he had to go (that was only the second thing I had understood). The hostess of the party told me later that he had thoroughly enjoyed talking to me and, 'What a nice conversationalist' I was! I had, in fact, resorted to nodding and shaking my head and praying that the noises I made were all in the right places. To this day I don't know what he said.

## Learn the art of conversation

There are, as I found out that evening, many Christians who have no difficulty at all in communicating confidently through their speech. (I assume the young man was a Christian!) It is worth saying, however, that if that is the case it's a good thing to check before God that our speech isn't too confident. There's nothing worse than an arrogant Christian. Our confidence must be a humble one which comes from the knowledge of what we are in Christ, not a puffed-up image about ourselves.

Learning the art of conversation can take us a long way in getting to know and serve others and it is worth taking the trouble to develop it as a skill. Many Christians are not prepared to hold 'superficial' conversations with others. They feel they are wasting their time if they are not talking about God or about related issues. Yet often it is a superficial conversation which can win the confidence of someone we want to get to know.

At a dinner party I held some time ago I had invited a few friends, including an unbelieving neighbour. I wanted to get to know her but had never had the opportunity yet of talking about Christ. I didn't feel that the time was right and yet I wanted more contact with her. She came to the dinner party and seemed to settle in very quickly and make friends with the other guests. I was concerned because the level of conversation that evening was very superficial indeed. We hardly discussed anything serious and I felt that it might have been a waste of time. Two days later, I received a letter from my neighbour. She thanked me for the evening, saying that it was just what she needed to be able to relax and chat and enjoy herself. In fact she went to great lengths to say how much she appreciated it. So much so, that she wanted me to go and have a meal with her. I had to read the letter three times before I could fully take in what she said. How could she have possibly enjoyed herself? I had found it quite a superficial, even boring evening and yet it meant a lot to her. Are we prepared to be bored and superficial in order to make contact with our unbelieving friends?

It is worth remembering, however, that in the process of developing our skills of speech and conversation we can get ourselves involved in arguments. Once we start to argue, up go the barriers and communication channels get blocked. Arguing never achieves anything except the satisfaction of knowing that we have either won our case or we have made someone else look silly, both of which are totally unacceptable for the Christian. There are ways of holding a conversation without falling into the trap of arguing. Finding as much common ground as possible is a help. Beginning a sentence with, 'Well, that may be true in such and such a circumstance' or, 'That's possible, but have you thought of . . .' might work too, particularly if the discussion is on a subject you feel you do know something about. But at all costs don't argue!

That doesn't mean, however, that we cannot have a sensible conversation. By avoiding arguments we are not necessarily agreeing with what the other person is saying. Someone once told me that the Christians she had known were 'soft' because they always wanted to agree with everyone in order to keep the peace. (I could have told her that many of the Christians I knew were a pain in the neck because they insisted on being right!) Keep the peace we must, but we should certainly not agree with everyone. Healthy, buoyant conversation can be a very stimulating experience. 'Agreeing to differ' is perhaps a helpful principle to bear in mind. We can differ from someone without being argumentative. We can agree that we have different opinions and give each other the freedom to state those opinions and to discuss them maturely. There is very rarely any benefit in the Christian winning an argument. Nothing is achieved by it except perhaps that you get a name for being pig-headed.

## Be up-to-date

Perhaps one of the most important things we can do to ensure that we always have something to talk about, as I mentioned earlier, is to be up-to-date on current affairs. Some years ago when Britain was in the grip of a very serious power strike, a few of us Christians were chatting at a coffee evening. Someone mentioned the strike and how very serious it was getting. One of the people present said, 'What strike is that?' I was shocked. The papers had been full of it. Each radio news bulletin had given coverage of the latest developments. It seemed that everyone in Britain was concerned except this one person who obviously had not heard the radio nor read a newspaper for at least three weeks. If we do not know what is going on in the world around us, how can we possibly communicate that we care about the world we're living in? This person was very involved in the church and probably each evening would have been taken up with Christian work. It may have been better perhaps if one of those evenings had been given to reading the paper and catching up on the week's news. The old saying, 'He's so heavenly minded that he's no earthly use' is a good one to remember. People in the world today are concerned about the future; they are concerned about the economy; about political strain between countries; about international unrest. Perhaps more than anything, they are concerned about how all of these things affect them and their children.

One Sunday afternoon I was talking to some young people who brought up the subject of nuclear weapons. Each one of them was very concerned and frightened at the prospect of nuclear war. They were very well-informed about the various development programmes in both the Soviet Union and the United States, far more so than I was. It is vital that we know what is going on in the world around us in order to care and then influence in whatever way God intends for us. If we slip away from that level of communication, another channel is blocked, and it is adding more fuel to the unbeliever's idea that

Christians can't talk about anything but God.

But Christians can talk about many things and we can take a stand on some of these issues. We can have convictions and informed opinions about them.

What do you think about nuclear weapons? about abortion? about unilateral disarmament? about keeping the weapons race going in order to provide a deterrent? about genetic engineering? about euthanasia? These are all very valid, controversial and emotive issues in today's world. People are looking for answers to these questions. They are looking for people who can take a stand and who know what they believe. This doesn't mean that we should force our opinions on others but we can and should confidently state what we feel about particular issues.

Reading the editorials in good newspapers, watching documentary programmes on television, talking to people who are an authority on a given subject in order to find out more – all these can help us to be able to discuss confidently the issues of the world today.

In a similar vein, we Christians can work on becoming interesting people to talk to. It helps to be knowledgeable in just one or two subjects. One of my favourite interests is civil aviation. A strange interest for a woman, perhaps, but it is something that I am keenly interested in. I enjoy looking at the social development of aviation and the history of how the concept of civil flying has come about. Once I was at a dinner with several people whom I didn't know. Most of them were men. The conversation had been quite heavy going and I was wondering how long we could go on with the niceties of polite chat. Then, one of the men asked if anyone knew the latest news on the DC-10 groundings. The DC-10, a wide-bodied aircraft, had been grounded because of some serious questions about the mounting of the engines. One of the other men made some comment about what he had heard. I was able to join in the conversation confidently. I knew what the latest status was on the problems of the DC-10 and I was able to talk intelligently about the aircraft. My male companions were very surprised but it did start a conversation far more meaningful than had previously been the case. We talked for a good twenty-five minutes about the DC-10's problems and what the possibilities were for solving them. Communication channels were opened up. I found I was listened to and my opinions were asked. Being knowledgeable on one or two subjects demonstrates that you have taken the trouble to think seriously about something.

## Express concern

Verbal communication is a great medium for getting to know what people's needs are. You learn so much by asking questions. Asking someone, 'How are you?' will usually get the response, 'Oh, I'm OK'. But if we ask something more specific, such as, 'How's your wife these days?' or, 'How are your children doing?', then we get a much more specific answer.

I have to work at remembering the facts that people have given me. It is something that I have had to pray for because I forget very quickly not only names of people, which can be very embarrassing, but also basic facts about them or things they have done. A friend of mine had had a pleasant conversation with someone he met. A year later, my friend met the same lady again. As they were chatting she said to him, 'How are your two little boys?' He was amazed that she had remembered that he had two sons. It meant a lot to him and he opened up and told her how they were getting on and the things he was concerned about for them.

It's a way of showing care, especially when we remember details, and particularly if that detail has been a problem or a concern. If a colleague has a sick child, then to ask them some time later how the child is getting on can be a way of expressing love.

God can give us a spirit of discernment to spot areas of need where we can not only show Christian love but also enter a deeper level of communication. It is always encouraging to someone who has a problem when someone else is prepared to share their own problems and needs. So many of us, I feel, are afraid to share failures. We only want to share successes and to tell how God has changed us, but we are more real as people if we can admit that we too have struggles and admit those struggles while we are going through them, not after God has given us the victory. The difference is that believing and unbelieving friends alike can see us struggling in company with God and can be encouraged as they see God give us victory *in* the problem.

The world needs to see the Christian going through these struggles. How many times does the unbeliever ask, 'Well, if God exists, why is there so much trouble in the world and why do people have so many problems?' If we do not communicate that we Christians have just the same kind of problems and pressures as unbelievers do, then what do we have to offer, except a 'pie in the sky when you die' kind of Christianity? But if we can demonstrate that God is in those battles with us, then it is yet another opportunity to show how his power is made perfect in our weakness and how he meets us in our needs. It's a big challenge to take on. It's much easier to keep our mouths shut until we've 'got the victory' and then talk about it!

## Watch your sense of humour

There are few things more undesirable or irritating than someone whose speech is never serious. A sense of humour is a God-given quality which, when used properly, can be an invaluable asset to effective communication, but there are many Christians who seem to think that it is a virtue to play amateur comedian, whether or not they have a captive audience!

Some years ago I was spending a relaxing evening with some friends at their home. We had just finished dinner when someone from my friends' church called to deliver something. He was introduced to me, along with the other guests, but he refused to be serious. After making some silly comment to each of us he proceeded to tell us all the 'funny' things that had happened to him that week. The stories were interspersed with jokes which were as 'funny' as his stories.

He stayed about half an hour and upon his departure we all breathed heavy sighs of relief!

We must ask God and ourselves if our humour serves others. If it does not, then we should do something about it very quickly. I couldn't help thinking how much more effective that young man's communication could be if only he would be a little more serious.

Someone told me once that he had realized how much he used his humour to draw attention to himself. 'I suddenly became aware I was in fact feeding my ego. I enjoyed being the centre of attention.' This particular person handled his problem maturely. Rather than deciding 'never to tell another joke', he simply became more thoughtful of others and more considerate about the timing of his humorous contributions! He became an attractive and pleasant man to be with. Now his sense of humour really does serve others because he has asked God to help him use it for his glory.

Paul tells us that there should be no 'foolish talk or coarse joking' (Ephesians 5:4). The context of the passage is impurity but I believe the principle is also applicable to what I am saying. 'Foolish talk and coarse joking' cannot possibly help anyone. They will probably do the opposite. Nor do they glorify the God who gave us our sense of humour.

Through that faculty we call speech, we can love, care, impart knowledge, communicate the love of God. Let us therefore ask the Creator God to give us the grace and wisdom we need to use it to glorify him.

# Don't be Afraid to Think

Richard came up to me and began to tell me about his difficulties in relating to other Christians in his fellowship. I was surprised because he was a pleasant young man with a likeable manner and an attractive sense of humour. As his story unfolded, however, I began to understand his problem. 'The Christians I know tell me that I'm rebellious,' he explained. 'They say I shouldn't ask so many questions and should just get on with being a Christian.' Richard didn't seem at all rebellious to me. Quite the opposite in fact. Then he said something which hit the nail on the head. 'I have tried to explain to them that I can't really get to know God for myself unless I'm prepared to think and ask questions to gain understanding.'

My heart went out to him. He was a fine young man with a genuine desire to serve God with all his heart and get to know him better. Yet because he had a keen and questioning mind he was branded 'rebellious'. Understandably, he was fast becoming disillusioned with his new-found faith.

## Mind versus the Holy Spirit?

Sadly, this is not an isolated case. There seems to be an attitude in some Christian circles that using the mind that God has given us is somehow denying the freedom of the Holy Spirit to teach us directly. Nothing could be further from the truth. In the book of Matthew, Jesus himself states categorically that we must among other things, love God with all our mind (Matthew 22:37). It is in fact the 'first commandment'. This surely means that just as with anything else entrusted to us by God, we are to be good stewards of that faculty we call the mind; developing it, using it to increase our understanding of God and what he requires of us.

The dangers inherent in the attitude encountered by Richard are many. One of these is something I have already made reference to: the danger of legalism. The alternative to thinking for ourselves is that someone else does it for us. Opinions are passed down to younger Christians as scriptural truth, with the result that believing they should submit to their elders, young Christians are taking on pre-digested opinions as part and parcel of Christian living. This ultimately gives rise to a culture in which a kind of unspoken policy reigns. Certain things are 'done' or 'not done' in such a culture. Where Scripture is clear on a subject then this is fine, but where it is not clear then it can be very dangerous indeed, because it becomes very easy to make assumptions on behalf of the group which in fact may not necessarily be right for everyone.

I believe that one of the reasons why God has given us the ability to think is because he has created each of us as unique individuals. That uniqueness permeates every area of our lives, including the way we interpret Scripture for ourselves, for our own individual walk with God. It is easy, perhaps, to think that Scripture is unclear because of some problem in translation, or because some vital passage is missing. And yet if we believe that 'all Scripture is inspired by God' (2 Timothy 3:16 RSV) then we must recognize that this 'inspiration' also embraces those parts of God's word which are, seemingly, unclear. He has given us minds so that we can work at them and find some help, even from the toughest sections of the Bible.

## The renewing of your mind

Rather than passing on to younger Christians pre-digested opinion, should we not be helping them dig deeply into Scripture for themselves, teaching them to ask the questions that will reveal the truth to them individually? Shouldn't the church be fulfilling its responsibility to them by helping them to glorify God by walking in faith? Perhaps the reason why we don't do this is because we have never learned to do these things for ourselves. Perhaps we have grown up in such a culture, eating pre-digested food and afraid of stepping over the boundaries of unspoken policy, never questioning, never taking the risk of being misunderstood. Where Scripture is clear, we must obey. But within the clarity of the black-and-white laws in its pages there is freedom to discover, with God's help, what our own convictions should be, how we should behave, in those areas that are not so black-and-white. It is the obedience to the clear which enables us to act in faith in the unclear. The Living Bible's paraphrase of

Psalm 119:45 illustrates the point I am making: 'May I never forget your words for they are my only hope' (the black-and-white laws of Scripture); 'therefore I will keep on obeying you forever and forever, free within the limits of your laws . . .' (the not so black-and-white).

Within the clear boundaries of God's laws there is freedom. Not a freedom to be used as a licence to sin, but to please God in our own individual way. How wise of our Heavenly Father to give us that freedom. How it must please him to see his children seeking his guidance and obeying, in faith, in their own unique way.

Another danger associated with a lack of thinking, and one which is perhaps a consequence of legalism, is that we become judgmental. The man-made laws of the kind of unspoken policy mentioned above will invariably be violated by those who refuse to be drawn into its net. It is then that a fellowship rises in judgment, accusing the victim of sin, while in his own heart he has taken an obedient step of faith.

Learning to think and use our minds takes effort. But if we don't do it then we will remain dependent on others for our behavioural codes, with all the consequences that brings. God, in his wisdom, gave you and me a unique identity. The moulding of that identity in accordance with God's will begins in the mind. How can I then be the person God intended me to be if I don't use the mind he intended me to use in order to work out the 'moulding process' for myself? Paul makes reference to this in Philippians when he encourages the young church to 'work out [their] salvation with fear and trembling' (Philippians

2:12). The apostle clarifies his statement by explaining, 'For it is God who works in you to will and to act according to his good purpose' (verse 13).

We often forget that God is committed to transforming us into the image of his Son. That commitment manifests itself in the power, mercy and forgiveness he has made available to us. But we must recognize that the transformation begins in the mind. It is there that God intends the transforming work to begin. In Romans 12 we see another pearl of wisdom from the pen of Paul: 'Do not conform any longer to the pattern of this world, but be transformed by the renewing of your mind. Then you will be able to test and approve what God's will is – his good, pleasing and perfect will' (Romans 12:2).

The more we learn to study the Scriptures for ourselves, the more we will be able to surrender to the 'moulding' God has in mind for us. It is our responsibility to do all we can to increase our intake of Scripture. Bible study on a regular basis together with others is a fundamental requirement. In addition to this, our own daily times with God should include some meditation (thinking around) some passage of the Bible, asking ourselves questions to reveal truth: What is this passage saying? What can it mean? What is God saying? How should I respond? As we begin to obey what God asks of us in these times, our thinking will gradually change to come more in line with God's thinking. Our minds will be transformed because we are allowing God to *renew* them.

# Stepping-stones to understanding

Christians who refuse to think are unattractive
Christians. I can think of several I know who have
tragically received the reputation of being 'boring'. How very sad this is. And yet it is their own
doing. They will not take the time to ask pertinent
questions about Scripture and how it can apply to
the needs of today's world. They scan a newspaper but fail to form convictions and opinions
that could stimulate conversation with
unbelievers. Rather than use the happenings of
the world around them as stepping-stones to
understanding its desperate need for God, they
turn away shocked and fearful and unable to face
reality. That fear kills the spontaneity that God
gave them along with their uniqueness. They
become predictable and boring. What a tragic witness to the beauty and magnificence of God.

If we are to be real people, individual people,
functioning in our uniqueness, then we must be
prepared to think. We must ask God to protect us
from the sin of presumption and ask him to give
us the ability to think laterally: to think around a
subject in order to gain understanding. We live in
a world which desperately needs the saving
power of Christ. Only as we, the ambassadors of
that priceless message, come to terms with what
is required of us while we are in the world can we
ever hope to communicate that saving power in
its fulness, in its true dynamism.

Having said all of that, however, I am only too
aware that there are many Christians in the world
today who have the very opposite kind of problem. They think too much! By that I mean that by

over-analysing situations, people or even Scripture itself, they run the risk of closing up the channels of the mind and heart which should always be open and seeking opportunities for faith. The mind should be used to deepen our understanding, not to dissect it. A young woman once told me that she could not understand how she could be sure of her salvation while her thoughts were often so sinful. She had tried in several ways to analyse the truth that her salvation was given to her by grace and not as a result of her own efforts. Each time she came to the same conclusion: 'I'm not good enough, therefore I don't deserve it, therefore I shouldn't have it, therefore I can't believe it!'

It was so sad to see this young Christian struggling on this and many other issues. She was using her mind in the wrong way. She was approaching scriptural truth from a human standpoint, desperately trying to gain some intellectual satisfaction from the things she found difficult, rather than acknowledging that however good a mind she might have, there comes a point at which the thinking must stop and faith must begin. Someone once said, 'What I understand, I believe; what I don't understand, I believe by faith.' There are times when God calls us to sink our intellectual pride and come to him as a little child. It is then that faith is given a chance.

It is an indescribable privilege to have been given a unique identity. That privilege contains what is perhaps an even greater one, that the moulding and development of that identity toward the ultimate goal – Christlikeness – was designed to be shared with us as a joint responsibility with God.

We obey, God moulds. As our minds are renewed, re-educated, re-charged through obedience to the word of God, the transformation process begins. 'Then you will be able to test and approve what God's will is – his good, pleasing and perfect will' (Romans 12:2).

# Glad to be Sexual

'So God created man in his own image, in the image of God he created him; male and female he created them' (Genesis 1:27).

Adult sexuality is the dimension of our lives which shows the difference between a man and just an overgrown boy, a woman and just an overgrown girl. It is a wonderful dimension, and it is certainly one which infiltrates every other area. It affects the way we think and speak, our relationships, our ambitions. (Part of sexuality involves the physical sex drive. I will discuss that separately.) Right across the board, sexuality is a vital and wonderful part of us.

In the Christian world, it is something which is often neglected, feared or even ignored. How do *you* view your sexuality, the fact that you are a man or a woman? Do you ever think about it? Or is it something that you simply take for granted? 'I was born a little boy and therefore I am now a man.' 'I was born a little girl and therefore I am now a woman.'

## Accepting adulthood

Do we look and carry ourselves like the men and women we are? Obviously sexuality does not begin at puberty. Little boys are not identical to little girls, but fully becoming an adult is bound up with becoming a consciously sexual adult. So many of the problems we face with our sexuality stem perhaps from the fact that we have not recognized that first and foremost, we are adults. Until we fully realize that, in every sense of the word, we will never come to terms with our sexuality.

I knew someone many years ago who admitted that she did not really want to be an adult. She didn't like the fact that she was plagued with adult sins. She didn't like the adult world she moved in, nor the conflicts and adult responsibilities that were a part of that. Consequently her mannerisms were girlish. She was immature in her behaviour. She used to collect fluffy toys and little girls' trinkets. She would refer to herself as a 'kid' and made it clear that she was irritated if she was referred to as anything but a child. And yet this person had a very bright mind. When I knew her she was twenty-seven years old. We talked about these things and I remember that on one occasion she became quite heated as she told me, 'I just do not *want* to be grown up.' I felt very sad for her and wondered why someone should ever feel that way. Unable to face up to reality, her reason I think was perhaps fear, linked with an unwillingness to step out in faith, trusting God to be with her as she matured into adulthood.

Becoming an adult is a traumatic process, and one which we all go through. We leave the protection of our homes where decisions are taken for us and on our behalf. We move from school to work or perhaps we go to college. Later we get married and a whole new set of responsibilities comes our way. We may buy a house. More responsibilities in the financial realm. We have children of our own. Again, a different set of questions, worries, conflicts. In the world today there are many, many pressures which are very cleverly designed to tempt the adult mind and to lead it into even more kinds of responsibilities that perhaps we would be better without.

But if we are going to function effectively as Christian people, we must learn to function as grown-up people, who are controlled by the living God, through the power of the Holy Spirit. Only when we do that can we have a sound basis on which to develop our sexuality. Sexuality cannot be built on a child's world. And yet if we look around us we see evidence of this very thing. We see the results of sexual immaturity: broken marriages, broken families, promiscuity, the inability to relate maturely to the opposite sex.

As Christians we have everything we need to 'grow up'. Because it is what God requires, he has given us every resource to become mature:

> Until we all reach unity in the faith and in the knowledge of the Son of God and become mature, attaining to the whole measure of the fulness of Christ. Then we will no longer be infants, tossed back and forth by the waves ... Instead, speaking the truth in love, we will in all things grow up into him who is the Head, that is, Christ (Ephesians 4:13–15).

In order to live with sexuality maturely, we must first be mature people. Intake of the word of God, together with daily application of its truths to our lives, is the only way to 'grow up into him, the Head'. The world gives much attention to the so-called virtues of 'sexual maturity' but for the Christian it is the maturity of his relationship to the risen Lord that is his priority. As this maturity begins to infiltrate his life, he is much more able to tackle sexuality issues effectively.

Often our need is to believe that God can and will enable us to integrate into the adult world. It might be helpful to list the aspects of the 'grown-up life' that we find difficult to handle and bring these one by one to God to ask that his power might be released within them. This might well be enough to free us from fear of certain aspects of adulthood, responsibilities, relationships and so on. But if there is a more serious problem, it might be necessary to talk to someone else, perhaps a minister or counsellor, who can help to pinpoint your difficulties.

Someone else I know experienced shyness and insecurity when in conversation with other people. As a result, he would resort to joking and teasing, which would bring the conversation down to a more childish level, at which he felt more comfortable. Once he realized his problem he asked God for wisdom to put it right. As he prayed, several points came to mind. Firstly, part of the reason for his shyness was a poor understanding of his worth as an individual to God. 'Why should people be interested in talking to *me*?' could sum up his feelings about himself. Praying that God would implant in his heart the truths of 1 Peter 2:9–10 helped considerably: 'A royal priesthood, a chosen people . . . I am chosen'.

Secondly, he realized that he did not have any particular opinions or convictions of his own. This, very naturally, made it almost impossible to have a sensible discussion with him. He decided to read the newspapers more thoroughly and to ask God to develop his thinking into clearer opinions and views. In addition to these points he also felt that he wasn't 'manly' enough. He thought that others would notice this and therefore not take him seriously anyway. This was in fact true. He asked God to make him literally more manly in his behaviour and appearance. He changed the way he wore his hair and was more careful about his clothes. This all helped to enhance his masculinity. He is an excellent example of how weakness, or human frailty, can be brought to God to have his power made perfect within it. As my friend's confidence grew, he became more and more encouraged to tackle other areas by faith. He is convinced that the change is because he has allowed God's power to infiltrate those areas he had once ignored or hidden away.

## Accepting gender

Perhaps one of the most distressing things to contend with in the area of sexuality is the problem of feeling a foreigner in your own gender. It is not uncommon for men to feel that they 'should have been born female' and vice versa. I have come across this phenomenon more than once and it certainly can cause a great deal of heartache and sadness. To know that one is stuck with a body which physically seems so alien to what one feels can lead many a Christian to despair. It can, if not brought before God, cause resentment and bitterness, simply because, physically, there is no way out. This phenomenon also often manifests itself in physical attraction for the same sex, thereby opening up opportunity for homosexual practice. (I should clarify here that not all homosexually orientated people experience the conflict of 'wrong gender'.)

The world tells us to 'be what we feel we are'. But if we are developing a daily and stable walk with God then we see things from a very different point of view. We are able, by faith, to see potential problems as areas of potential victory. This may sound trite and pious but it is true.

Let us look at the issue in the light of Scripture. Genesis tells us that when God created man and woman he drew a clear distinction between the two genders. 'Male and female he created them' (Genesis 1:27). We are born either male or female, one *or* the other. In very exceptional circumstances, there may be a genital abnormality at birth which may require surgery to bring the person within one gender. These cases, thankfully, are extremely rare and account for a fraction of the percentage of infant disability.

If you are genitally and bodily properly formed and your reproductive processes function normally, then you are either male or female. The fact that you may not *feel* that is another issue. Those I have known with this problem who have peace about their circumstances have all chosen to act, by faith, on what they know to be true – despite what they feel. They have accepted that they have been created either male or female and whichever they are, they have actively developed themselves according to that gender. A female acquaintance has spent time developing feminine mannerisms in order to counteract her masculine ones (though these come more naturally to her). She began to wear less masculine clothes and styled her hair. She became more careful about the way she sat, stood, carried herself. Although she would admit that she still feels more of an affinity with men, she has become an attractive woman, encouraged by the victory she has seen God give in her weakness. Because her behaviour is now in line with what God created her to be, she has gained in confidence. For her, too, the key was to take hold of scriptural truth and act upon it.

In certain cases the problem may seem too overpowering to deal with alone. If this is your experience, I would recommend counselling with a reputable and Scripture-based Christian counsellor who will be able to help and support you as you face the issue with God. Just remember – you are part of a chosen race, a royal priesthood. You have received mercy. You are one of God's people. You have every reason to be confident that God will enable you to integrate well and confidently with those around you.

# Relating to the opposite sex

One of the problems facing Christians today is their ability or inability to relate to the opposite sex. Mistakes are made all the time, at both ends of the pendulum's swing, from prudishness and total ignorance of the opposite sex to sexual immorality and promiscuity.

Before discussing this any further, it is worth reminding ourselves of the standards God has laid down for us in the sexual realm. In Paul's first letter to the Corinthians he makes it clear that sex is something which requires special mention: 'Flee from sexual immorality. All other sins a man commits are outside his body, but he who sins sexually sins against his own body. Do you not know that your body is a temple of the Holy Spirit, who is in you . . . you were bought at a price. Therefore honour God with your body' (1 Corinthians 6:18–20). It is imperative that we decide in our hearts and minds that *sexual sin is forbidden*. As long as we tamper with thoughts of, 'What can I get away with?', whether in thought or action, we will never be in a position to experience either God's victory over sexual sin or his power working within our sexuality toward positive and constructive ends.

Once this is established, however, we can begin asking God for wisdom in relating to our brothers or sisters in Christ, thus enhancing our own sexuality. If the two sexes are separated for any length of time then we miss the wonderful complementary influence that one sex has upon the other.

We have a unique contribution to make to the opposite sex. If God had intended us all to be of only one gender he would have designed us that way. In my job, I find that most of my peers are men and I really enjoy working with them. For a short period of time I was in a work situation in which all my colleagues were women. It was very refreshing to come back into a mixed environment again. Men and women are different and we should be thankful for those differences and enjoy them as they complement our own lives.

Look at the life of Jesus, and the way he related to both men and women. There were many women among his followers who were devoted to him and who obviously felt as comfortable with him as he did with them. There is no evidence anywhere in the gospels to indicate that Jesus was ill at ease with either believing or unbelieving women. And yet if Scripture is true we must accept that he was a man in every sense of the word. Scripture tells us that he was 'in all points tempted as we are'. And yet he remained sinless.

He was often to be seen in the company of prostitutes. He went to functions, weddings, where there would be a mixture of people, a cross-section of the society of the day, and yet he never appeared to be either shocked, uncomfortable or ill at ease.

Because we have the Holy Spirit of God living within us, we can trust him to give us that ability to relate to our male or female counterparts in a relaxed, comfortable and serving way. Unfortunately we sometimes relate too well to the opposite sex and find ourselves with problems and relationship difficulties, or we relate so badly that we have hang-ups and fears and always feel uncomfortable.

But when we remind ourselves that we are members of God's royal family, let us also remember that our male or female opposites are also part of that family. We are part of one another with a unique contribution to make to one another.

# Complementarity and friendships

The problem is not limited to the Christian world. The feminist movement has gained much support over the past decade, partly as a result of this very difficulty. While much good is done through the movement and women have been helped tremendously to take their rightful place alongside men in the world, in industry and in business, a woman can greatly impair what I believe is God's objective for her – complementing her male counterparts – by trying to compete with men. I am always thrilled to hear of women who have achieved success in the world, but I am equally saddened by those successful women who have got where they are by acting in a masculine way in their dealings with other people and in their communication with them. At the risk of being controversial, I would suggest that if a woman cannot achieve success without taking on male characteristics, then perhaps success should not be hers anyway.

The male and female characteristics are there to complement one another. Trying to be a member of the opposite sex, for whatever reason, is in a sense denying what God has made us in his perfect will and wisdom. As men and women we need one another to realize fully our own sexuality.

I know several Christians who readily admit that they have no friendships with the opposite sex. They have acquaintances, contacts whom they perhaps meet at church or during their Bible study fellowships, but they don't really have friends. I would encourage anyone to develop friendships with both men and women. If we walk by faith, then we can trust God to keep our minds and our thoughts under his control as we get to know our friends. If we don't learn to do this then we will be encouraging a 'separatist' kind of existence, which is not only unnatural but can lead to an unhealthy pattern of thinking.

Young Christians coming into that kind of context will inherit their spiritual parents' separatist attitude. I wish I had five pounds for every time I have heard either a man or a woman say, 'Well, it's difficult talking to girls' or, 'It's difficult talking to men, because I never know what they are thinking about me.' There has to be an element of trust. Many times I have found myself in conversation with a man and been very aware of the fact that he would rather be somewhere else. He has communicated a discomfort in talking with a woman. Perhaps he is worried about his mind and he is anxious to keep himself from sinning. That's fine, but how is he making *me* feel?

I have heard it said that it is better for young men and women not to engage in deep conversation with one another because of the temptations that this close communication can bring. There may be an element of truth in that, but where is the element of *trust*? Where is faith? A young man once told me that he always felt uncomfortable talking to girls because he felt they were preoccupied by thoughts of, 'Is he the right one?' or, 'Am I attracted to him, I wonder if he likes me?' I have every sympathy with him. Surely, as adults, we should rather be asking ourselves, am I serving that other person, am I putting them at their ease? Or am I too concerned with my mind and whether it's pure or whether it's impure, whether my thoughts are of marriage or whether I am worried about being tempted? We can surely ask God to give us the ability to treat people as people. We need to be able to sense whether we are serving them or not in our conversation with them. If the person we are talking to is of the opposite sex then that's an added bonus. Enjoy it and so will he/she. Ask God to take the pressure off!

## Roles

Men and women are often afraid of passing compliments to one another. Like most people, I love receiving compliments. It makes me feel more confident, it makes me feel appreciated. Complimenting each other in an adult way communicates that we appreciate the other person and that we notice things about them. There is no need to be overly aware of details about others, but the occasional compliment can encourage someone tremendously.

For purely chemistry reasons, it means more to me to receive a compliment from a man than from a woman! I am sure that men, similarly, appreciate a compliment from a woman far more than from one of the guys at work. Thank God for that chemistry! It was created by the Creator of all; by the King of Kings and the Lord of the universe. It's a perfect chemistry, and God has ordained that we enjoy it.

I am often asked how I feel about chivalry. I personally appreciate a man who is courteous and chivalrous to me and I know many men who would be very uncomfortable if they were prevented from being that way.

But a word to the women. If a man shows you courtesy, perhaps by opening the door for you, do please say 'thank you'. I have seen many walk through doors that have been held open for them by some courteous man and they never even turn to acknowledge him, let alone thank him.

A word to the men. In these days of equality, it could be that you will be working with or living near women who do not appreciate men who display that kind of courtesy. On more than one occasion I have seen a man made to feel very foolish by a woman who did not appreciate a courteous gesture. For your own protection, be sensitive about women like this. You can usually tell if a woman prefers not to be treated in that way. In which case, she can hold the door open for you!

I heard a lovely story recently about a young man who was in a department store during his lunch hour. On his way out of the store he noticed a smart lady approaching the door at the same time. He stood back and opened the door to let her go through first. She turned to him and, looking very irritated and angry, said, 'I do hope you didn't open that door for me because I'm a lady!' To which he replied, 'Oh no madam, not because you are a lady, but because I am a gentleman!'

Whatever our views on the male/female role, and I am not saying that one is more right than the other, we simply need to be sure it is what God wants us to do. And whatever we have chosen, we must serve one another in that, and respect one another's views.

How much do we work on enhancing our sexuality? It saddens me tremendously when I look around at the people I work with, at the people I see on the street, the people in my neighbourhood, many of whom appear to be 'sexless'. Unfortunately, many Christians too fall into this category, afraid to develop their manliness or their womanliness. Just as I was afraid before I was a Christian to stand out in a crowd and so I would wear drab clothes, many Christians, too, because of the fear of appearing too aware of their sexuality, go too far the other way and communicate nothing of it at all. Like every other aspect of our lives, we are stewards of our sexuality. Just as we prayerfully consider how to be good stewards of other things in our lives, we should be prayerfully considering how to develop our sexuality to be glorifying to God and a vital channel of communication to others.

## The problem with temptation

What about this fear of temptation from the opposite sex? I have heard young men say, 'I can't keep my mind pure because of what the girls in my fellowship are wearing. They look too attractive, too tempting.' Similarly, I've heard girls say, 'The men are so good looking and so attractive that I really can't keep my mind on my Bible study.' Both sexes have a responsibility to serve one another here, just as in every other area of life. If what we wear is seductive and tempting, then we are not serving others. We could be causing them to sin. Having said that, however, I do not mean that we should be colourless, sexless lumps!

It is my responsibility, yes, not to behave or dress in any way which might prove tempting to a man. It is a man's responsibility similarly, not to do anything that will tempt a woman. But I am not *solely* responsible for the purity of a man's mind. He is too. Neither is a man solely responsible for the purity of a woman's mind. She is too. If we can develop a shared responsibility in this, then we will also develop a mutual trust and appreciation for one another as people.

Scripture teaches us that part of the fruit of the Spirit is self-control – not abstinence. We could run away from everything which might tempt us. But if we did that, we would run away from life itself. Life is full of temptation. Jesus lived in a world full of temptation, too, and yet he remained sinless because he kept close to the Father. I am always encouraged and challenged by some verses in Psalm 18: 'He fills me with strength and protects me wherever I go. He gives me the surefootedness of a mountain goat upon the crags. He leads me safely along the top of the cliffs' (verses 32–33, Living Bible).

A young man once told how God had freed him to enjoy girls simply because they are girls. 'I used to be so scared of sinning in my mind,' he said. 'Then God showed me that because I am a healthy male, it was natural that I should enjoy them, but not necessarily sin. I realized that there is a big difference between sinning in my mind (imagining sexual contact) and enjoying and appreciating women. God was asking me to exercise self-control – that is, control of my thoughts – by paying attention to the girl *as a person*, with an attitude of serving rather than getting. I soon began to feel much freer to enjoy relationships with the opposite sex.'

## What can I do with my sex drive?

The sex drive is a difficult thing to define. It is the energy, the dynamic, which gives us the appreciation of the opposite sex that we were talking about. Sometimes it's a nebulous swirling mass of energy that we don't know what to do with. It is the cause of the twinkle that appears in our eye when we appreciate something in a man or woman. It's the thing that gives us a sense of fun with the opposite sex. It's the dimension, which when linked with our emotions (as it is very closely) gives us the ability to appreciate deeply in our innermost being some of the beauties of life and relationships.

It is also very specifically the physical urge for sexual communication with another person. It is the physiological process, the series of chemical changes taking place in the body, which drives us to want to express what we feel for someone through sexual contact.

There is really only one way for the unmarried to deal with the specific physical urge. That is by prayer and by turning away from that which causes the urge. I should add, though, that for both men and women (and I have spoken to men about this), the urge which seems uncontrollable comes, usually, only if we have been stimulated. (It *can* appear for no apparent reason, but normally there has been some stimulus somewhere). In which case we have obviously been in some situation where we should not have been, for things to get to that point. In marriage, within the context of love, it is God's perfect will that the sex drive be satisfied. But I would add for those who are single, that if we never learn to control our sex drive outside of marriage, we will never learn to control it inside, where it is meant to serve our partner.

Be careful not to ignore your sexuality. It is one thing to accept it fully and decide firmly that you will control it: quite another to pretend it isn't there, try to live without it and push it down into the subconscious where it can do great damage.

## God wants to help!

Often, when we feel we are longing for sex, we are in fact longing for intimacy. Non-sexual, loving relationships on a deep level can be very fulfilling. God can give us an intimacy with our friends which is emotionally very satisfying. Because the emotional intimacy is there, we find that our so-called longing for sex in the general sense can wane because we are fulfilled in other ways.

I have known many Christian couples who had great difficulty in keeping their relationship pure before marriage because they never learned to control their sexuality as single people. They never learned to bring feelings one by one to God as the situations came along. They simply ignored them and pretended they weren't there. Then the explosion of sexual dynamic happened when they fell in love. They had battles and difficulties in maintaining a basic level of purity, to the point where the simple enjoyment of getting to know one another was spoiled by tension and frustration. Learning to control our sexuality through the power of God is far from easy, but it is a challenging and dynamic experience.

Perhaps part of the problem we have is that we don't know how each other's bodies function. Even today, in the 1980s, I am amazed at the ignorance of many Christians, even those who have had sexual experiences. A lack of knowledge can produce an unbalanced curiosity. It's worth praying about it and perhaps getting a good book (such as *Intended for Pleasure* by Ed and Gaye Wheat, published by Scripture Union) which would explain the functioning of the opposite sex. When the facts are understood, take them to God and leave them there and thank him that you now understand an important part of his creation.

When God created that part of us we call sex, it was perfect. And when we find ourselves attracted to someone, it is God's objective that it should remain sinless. It is Satan's objective to turn that situation into sin. By thanking God specifically for what we feel and how we respond, we lift the situation out of the domain of Satan and place it back into God's domain.

If you haven't already read the Song of Solomon and meditated upon it, I would strongly suggest that you do that. It is a beautiful account of the love between man and woman, but it also reflects the deep love God has for his children. It reflects the intimacy that we can have with God. The more we give ourselves to God in that intimacy, the more we allow him to infiltrate every area of our lives, including our sexuality, the more fulfilled we are going to be as people. If we remain unmarried, then we go through life enjoying the tremendous fulfilment of a deep relationship with God. If we marry, we take that fulfilment with us and we become a much richer marriage partner. Read the Song of Solomon slowly. I would suggest just a few verses every day. Meditate upon them and thank God for the depth of communication that he wants to have with us, and ask him specifically to show you how best to express your sexuality and how best to control it. He wants to help you. He certainly will if you really want to co-operate.

# CHAPTER ELEVEN

# Getting the Message Across

To the Jews I became like a Jew, to win the Jews. To those under the law I became like one under the law (though I myself am not under the law), so as to win those under the law. To those not having the law I became like one not having the law . . . so as to win those not having the law. To the weak I became weak, to win the weak. I have become all things to all men so that by all possible means I might save some (1 Corinthians 9:20–22).

In the previous chapters of this book we have looked at the potential which is ours if we have committed our lives to the Lord Jesus Christ. As we trust God to develop that potential and cooperate with him through faith and obedience we will begin to change. Even if we limit that development to just the six areas I have outlined, there will still be quite a transformation. The change in us will have two major consequences: it will bring glory to God, as sin and weakness bow to the victory Christ died to give; and it will have far-reaching effects in our communication. We will perhaps sense a greater confidence or experience a deeper desire to share the power of the change we have seen in our lives with those who do not know Christ. So we are going to be far more usable as channels for the gospel. Spreading the good news of Christ does not mean that we limit our activity to 'getting people converted'. If we are to be witnesses in the true sense of the word then we should be communicating his life-changing power at all levels of life, in fact the very things we are discussing in this book.

The average unbeliever of today has little or no understanding of spiritual things. We cannot and should not expect him to be on our wavelength. Words that you and I understand as being crucial to our salvation, such as 'faith' or 'sacrifice', will mean something very different to an unbeliever. He has a different frame of reference. We may say something which to us will be crystal clear but by the time it has been filtered through his frame of reference it will mean something altogether different to him. Part of our job, then, is to help those without Christ to build a 'filter' that will help them understand the message. We have some foundation work to do before we can build the house.

We must begin somewhere and so I have endeavoured, in these last two chapters, to give some very practical help in the specific skills needed in the communication of our faith.

## Find out where people are

The foundation work clearly begins with establishing where our level of communication should be pitched. It will vary according to the person we are talking to at a particular time. But it is vital to find out at the start where the unbeliever stands, how far he is from the cross and his response to all it represents.

As we considered earlier, people are much further away from understanding the cross than they were, say, twenty years ago. We must therefore go back and meet them at their level of need. It is a very common mistake to assume that the unbeliever will understand what we say. The only way we can really find out where unbelievers stand is to get to know them as people, to listen to what they say and perhaps, more importantly, to what they don't say.

People we are with all the time, our neighbours, colleagues, are communicating just as much as we are. We can ask God for the ability to tune in our antennae to what they are communicating, whether verbally or non-verbally. I am not suggesting that we play amateur psychologists. Let's leave that to the professionals who know what they're doing. I simply mean that we can learn a lot by listening and observing. Half the battle that we face in communicating the gospel is won by listening. Yet how often do we go in with both feet, only to realize that we have either jumped in too soon or are on the wrong track altogether?

One day I was chatting to a young man I came to know through my work. He began to talk about death and how everything comes to an abrupt end when we die. I thought, 'This is the moment to face him with the scriptural truths of death.' So I began to talk about eternal life and what Jesus offers to us if we trust in him. I told him that he needn't be afraid of death but that, for the Christian, death was merely the gateway to eternity with God. I got quite carried away and waxed eloquent about glory and the wonderful promise to be forever with God. He sat very quietly for about ten minutes and then said to me, 'Well, actually, I'm *not* afraid of death at all. I don't really concern myself with what comes afterwards. What I'm saying is, it's a shame if you have wasted your life and then come to the end of it, having achieved nothing.'

I felt rather stupid. I had not listened to what he was really saying. Neither had I listened to what he *wasn't* saying. I had latched on to a word that he had used several times – death – and assumed that because I had been afraid of death before I was a Christian, he meant the same thing. In actual fact the concern of his heart was not death at all, but life, and the quality of life. I missed the boat quite badly and felt that there was no point at that moment in going on. I could sense in him a slight irritation, so I changed the subject. But that can happen so easily, particularly if we project the things we have gone through and the concerns we have had, on to others. People turn to Christ for all kinds of reasons and to assume that we know what those reasons are, without checking thoroughly, can lead us into trouble. What I should have done was ask him questions about his concern and then more questions to find out the level of those concerns. And let him do the talking.

It is a constant effort for me to learn how to ask questions and to listen to the answers. So often my kind of listening is merely being silent until the other person has finished what they are saying. Then I jump in with my pearl of wisdom.

Finding out where people are on the road to the cross does not only involve finding out what they think about God. They may not think about him at all. It is also important to learn how to ask intelligent questions and interpret the answers about other issues in life.

I once talked to somebody who had no concern at all for people and freely admitted it. He was very good with animals and had many of his own. He said he found them easier to relate to than people and went into great detail to explain why animals were just as important, if not more so, than human beings. I found that rather difficult. What do you say to someone who doesn't have any care at all for people around him? After a time I learned that his convictions about animals had been fed by the fact that he had had a very difficult relationship in his younger days and had been hurt through it. There had also been incidents throughout his life where he had felt rejected by people. So bit by bit, the picture came together, the reason why he felt the way he did. I had actually started talking to him about God and we didn't get anywhere, simply because he had no belief, no acknowledgment at all of the existence of God. But when we began to talk about his own life and his own thoughts, we began to get somewhere – not very far, but somewhere!

I should like to suggest a little exercise that might be helpful in establishing where someone is on the road to the cross. Think of someone whom you're praying for and ask yourself the following question: Do I know where he or she stands? That is, do I know where that person is on the road to the cross? If the answer is 'yes', then ask yourself, 'What can I do to bring him or her just one step nearer?' It could be perhaps a further conversation about something that you have already discussed together. It could be that they are ready to read a book you would recommend. Not necessarily a Christian book but perhaps something that would help the development of their thinking just that little bit further. Perhaps they are ready to meet another Christian or even come to church with you. Whatever it is, pray that God would help you decide what you should do to bring that person just one step nearer than they already are.

If the answer to your original question is 'no', then ask yourself, 'Is there one thing I can do to find out a little bit more about where they are?' It could be simply to have coffee with them so that you can have a chat, depending on how well you know them. Or it may be you feel that you should ask some questions about something they may have said to you in the past. By taking the process one step at a time, we can trust God more easily. It is much more encouraging to ask God to help us just one step further than to pray that you would lead someone like that to Christ. That's a big thing to believe God for, particularly if that person has a long way to go before surrendering to him.

## Look for common ground

Once we have an idea where people are, then the next thing to do is look for common ground. The apostle Paul was an outstanding example of this. If we look back at the passage of Scripture at the beginning of this chapter, we see how hard he worked at keeping common ground when he was with unbelievers. Whether he was with Jews, Gentiles, or heathen, he maintained a certain level of agreement with them in order to keep lines of communication open. He got on their wavelength, as it were. Once we lose that common ground, then the barriers go up, and once that has happened they are very, very difficult to break down again. I think that the passage in 1 Corinthians is an encouraging one because Paul is pointing out that there are many things that we can do in order to keep that basic level of agreement. He adds, of course, that he must always do what is right as a Christian. But as long as we ensure that we are doing that, then there is a whole wealth of opportunities open to us to keep those communication channels with the unbeliever open. Part of this means that we are involved with unbelievers, on their terms. We will be talking more about that in the next chapter.

Common ground may be found by simply being with unbelievers and doing some of the things that they do, like joining clubs, societies, sports associations. Doing things together. They all help to establish contact. Mothers at home with young children have a natural link with other mothers who take their children to school at the same time.

But it isn't only the physical common ground. It is also the level of agreement that we must maintain in our conversations with unbelievers, and this is sometimes very difficult to do.

Have you ever been in a conversation with an unbeliever where he is explaining with great conviction and at great length the futility of believing in some basic Christian truth? If you're like me, then you find yourself, after the first few minutes, becoming more and more irritated and more and more determined to prove him wrong. Only a few days before writing this chapter, I found myself in a conversation just like that.

I was talking with an acquaintance who was telling me about her beliefs and her interpretation of Christianity. It had been a long time since I had heard anything so remarkably ridiculous. There were loopholes in just about everything she said and yet she was explaining all this to me with the attitude of, 'I will tell you because you really do need to know these things.' She felt sorry that I hadn't 'seen the light' as she had seen it. The more she went on, the hotter I became around the back of my neck. I began to feel the roots of my hair bristling. I told myself, 'Here is a poor lost soul whom you need to pray for and whom you need to understand and listen to.' What I *really* wanted to do was take her by the shoulders and shake her to shut her up. Well, 'in for a penny, in for a pound!' I thought. At the first pause in her exhortation I jumped in with both feet and began arguing with her. As you can imagine, it got me nowhere. It was only when I stopped and asked God to forgive me for my impatience and my pride in wanting to get my point across that things calmed down. We had to stop talking at that point. There was no use going on.

Since then we've chatted again quite pleasantly about it, but it reminded me that unless we can keep that vital common ground, the communication channels become blocked. If I had really prayed and thought and listened to what she was saying, then I would have seen that there were certain things that I *could* have agreed with and used as a springboard to say something else. But instead of that, I saw what she was saying as a barrage of foolishness and I reacted personally to it. To those readers who share my tendency to a quick temper, I say, I *do* know how you feel! But it can never please God if we argue.

It is true to say, however, that some unbelievers actually do want an argument. How often have you found yourself provoked by someone simply because they are wanting to get you mad or to trip you up? In situations like that it is probably better not to respond at all. They have temporarily shut the door at their end of the communication channel. It is no good for us to try to break that door down. The more we try, the more locks they will put on the other side. It is better to wait and pray that God will cause them to open the door again.

## Help people to see the implications of their statements

My conversation with my acquaintance leads me naturally on to the next point: help people to see the implications of what they say. Often an unbeliever takes great delight in telling you about some belief or opinion that he has, and yet he hasn't actually thought about the essence of what he is saying. This is an important area for us to look at because it is a step forward in helping the unbeliever to build the new frame of reference necessary for later understanding of the gospel itself.

I was talking one day with a colleague and the conversation turned to children. Suddenly she said, 'I don't believe that children should be brought up. I think that they should bring themselves up.' She went on to explain: 'The trouble with the world today is that adults have interfered with the development of children. Left to themselves, children would make a far better job of it.'

Now this was a sweeping statement and one which she obviously felt very strongly about. And she believed that she had certain facts to back up her opinion. But it was clear that she had never really stopped and *thought* about what she was in fact implying by her statement. I asked her, 'Do you mean then that the world would be a better place if children did not have any guidance from adults?'

She said emphatically, 'Oh, yes.'

I said, 'Are you saying then that man is basically good until he is interfered with?'

'Yes,' she said, 'I do believe that.'

I was stuck. I had never spoken to her about God in any detail. The only time I had ever mentioned his name, she had reacted negatively. I didn't know what to say. I prayed a desperate prayer: 'Please Lord, give me something to say to this girl.'

God answered that prayer and gave me something to say that I would never have thought of myself. I said to her, 'Let me ask you something. Imagine two toddlers in a playpen. There are no adults in their lives to interfere with them. Toddler 1 is playing with a bright red and yellow ball. What do you think is going to happen within a few minutes?'

My colleague said, 'Well, toddler 2 will try to take the ball away from him.'

I said, 'Then what will happen?'

'Toddler 1 will then try to grab the ball back again.'

I said to her, 'What do you think the outcome of that would be?'

She said, 'Oh, I suppose they would end up fighting over the ball. But that's healthy enough. The strongest one will win.'

I said to her, 'If you take that very same situation, add on thirty or so years and transplant it into an international setting, you have war.'

She looked at me and gulped. She said, 'I've never thought of it that way before.' She became very quiet and went back to her work.

God was very faithful in giving me something to say to that colleague. A few days later she and I were talking again and we were able to talk on a much more open level about God.

By helping people in this way we are gradually influencing their thinking. A new frame of reference is gradually being built in their mind. In time they will be ready to hear the specifics of the gospel and have something to relate them to.

Ros was telling me one day that she had had a similar experience in her office. There had been a general discussion during the lunch hour about morals. They had been trying to define what morality was. Someone had said that as long as you don't hurt anybody, you can do what you want. Another said that different groups of people had their own moral codes. Yet another said that the kind of person you're with at the time determines what is moral and what is immoral. Each opinion sounded very convincing. Ros had been quiet during all this discussion but she felt at this point it was time to say something, to help these colleagues to understand what they were actually implying. So she asked, 'Do I understand then that you feel that your morality is governed, to a large extent, by other people?'

'Yes,' was the reply. So Ros continued.

'Does this mean then that you can change your moral code depending on who you're with?'

'Yes,' was the reply again.

'Do you think, perhaps that could get rather confusing as to what is right or wrong for you personally, if you are having to change your behaviour in order to please a certain group of people at a certain time?' The office apparently became very quiet and no-one knew how to answer. Then one colleague said,

'Well, yes, I suppose it would get confusing. What do *you* think?' And Ros was given the perfect opportunity to explain what her convictions were about morals and was able to share something of the gospel. If she had gone in earlier, they might not have listened, but by helping them to see the implications of their statements she made them realize how very shaky was the foundation of their opinions.

Jim was talking to a colleague whom we shall call Michael. Michael began to tell Jim about what he called his 'philosophy of life'. He had spent a lot of time thinking about it and working out how man came to be. Michael has a brilliant mind and Jim felt rather swamped by his intellectual approach to the creation of life. He summed up by saying, 'I know you're a Christian, so you obviously believe that there's a God. I do not believe in the existence of any kind of intelligence at all outside of human intelligence. And even human intelligence is the result of cell formation in certain circumstances.'

Jim really didn't know how to answer and prayed the desperate prayer, 'Lord, help me to know what to say.' God did the usual thing and answered. Jim said, 'Michael, are you saying that you believe that even the intangible aspects of life come about because of purely physiological developments?'

And he said, 'Yes, I am saying that.'

Jim asked, 'Even things like love and hate?'

Michael was quite adamant. 'Oh, yes, they result from chemical and biological and physiological changes within the body.'

Jim was getting more desperate. He said, 'Do you believe, Michael, that in every man there is a sense of justice?'

He thought hard for a moment and then said, 'Yes, I think I do believe that.'

Jim said, 'Do you believe that an inborn sense of justice can be the result of physiological or chemical development?'

To which he replied, 'No, I don't think I can honestly say that. You've got me there.' Up to that point he had been convinced that he was right. There was no intelligence outside of human intelligence and even that was something which had evolved from purely physiological beginnings. Yet by that one question about a sense of justice, his whole theory was thrown into doubt and he had to think again.

Perhaps Michael was still a hundred miles from the cross but through that conversation he had been brought maybe two inches nearer, and two inches is better than nothing at all. With some people it is going to be a long, hard journey, but we can help them by learning to think with them and ask pertinent questions which challenge their assumptions.

# CHAPTER TWELVE

# Get Involved

## Tasty bait

It was a bright sunny day and Martin was feeling good. He parked the car at his office and went through the main entrance. Walking towards the lift, he saw a colleague coming down the stairs. Martin shouted a cheery, 'Good morning!'

The colleague, who also seemed to be in a pleasant mood that day, returned his greeting and said, 'What's making you so cheerful this morning?'

Martin said, 'Oh, good weather, good diet and God,' and proceeded to walk into the lift.

The colleague looked puzzled. 'And God?' he said.

'That's right,' said Martin. 'I'll tell you about it some day', closed the doors and off he went.

Later on that day, he met the same colleague again. 'What did you mean about God this morning?' he asked.

Martin replied, 'Oh, I just mean that life is so different if you have God in it with you', and carried on with what he was doing.

The colleague became more and more curious. 'Are you into God, then?' he said.

'Yes,' said Martin. 'Would you be surprised if I

said that he was the most important part of my life?'

'Oh,' said the colleague, 'I would.' This started a short conversation in which Martin very briefly explained that he was a Christian. This is what I call the art of dropping tasty pieces of bait. So often we feel we must come out with the whole story, the whole gospel, otherwise we fear that we are not successful in our communications with the unbelieving world.

I believe that God will help us if we ask him to drop tasty pieces of bait for people to bite, giving them just enough to make them curious, to make them want to know more. What Martin did was a good example of this and, knowing him, it was quite a deliberate tactic on his part. The whole of that morning the colleague he had greeted in the entrance had been thinking about what Martin had said about God. He was fascinated and, as the morning went on, became increasingly curious to know more about it. I feel it is important to add that Martin was very obviously sensitive to his colleague's mood. He knew he was in a good one. Had the colleague been feeling miserable that morning, it would have been inappropriate for Martin to have done what he did. But that sensitivity is something God can give us if we pray.

Some time ago a friend of mine told me that she was having difficulties in her marriage and we talked a lot about it. Up to that point, I had said very little about God. But I ended the conversation by saying, 'I believe in the power of prayer. I will pray for you.'

She looked mildly embarrassed and said quietly, 'Oh, thank you.'

The next time I saw her she said, 'Thank you for praying for me, I think it's working.' And she began to tell me more about her relationship with her husband and how things had improved slightly over the week. I didn't say anything more about prayer or about God but towards the end of our conversation, she said, 'Will you keep praying for me?' I said I would. Since then she has begun to ask questions about my faith and about God and has begun to think seriously for herself about the place that God can have in her life.

- One of the hardest things for us Christians to learn to do is to keep our mouths shut. But God will help us and will give us that sensitivity and skill to say just enough to create an interest. It is a skill and the more we practise it, in faith, the more skilful we will become. We will make mistakes, yes, but let's go out in faith, trusting God, and he will teach us how to whet people's appetites.

The Bible tells us, 'Seek and ye shall find.' Part of our job as Christians is to get people *wanting* to seek. I think dropping tasty morsels is part of that process. To get people seeking the truth. When they seek, they will find.

## Be shockproof

Perhaps one of the most difficult things required of us as we mix with unbelievers is that we be shockproof. The moment a Christian communicates shock, the communication channels are blocked. The unbeliever shuts the door and makes sure that it is well locked and bolted. It is very difficult not to show that we are shocked at some time in our life. The world is a nasty place and because our consciences have become sensitive through closeness to God, many things now appear distasteful to us. We become upset by the things that we see and the things people say. We are alarmed at happenings that the world accepts as the norm. And yet, if we are going to keep those communication channels open, then we must learn not to react openly to reveal our sense of shock.

I am always encouraged by the attitude of Jesus. Nowhere in the gospels is there any evidence that he ever appeared shocked. Jesus mixed with some of the most doubtful characters one could imagine. He dined with those whom many would consider to be the dregs of society. He was seen to be in the company of prostitutes and tax collectors. He must have seen and heard many things that would leave many a twentieth-century Christian speechless. And yet, although he was often saddened, he never reacted to anything that he saw or heard out of shock. In fact it is interesting to note that the only thing that he became really worked up about was lack of faith. It is very evident in the gospels that not only was Jesus prepared to be with people like this but he actually *wanted* to be with them. Jesus' secret lay in the fact that he looked at the sinner and not the sin. He looked at the person with needs rather than the needs themselves. We must ask God for that same ability and ask him to give us love for the sinner without condoning the sin.

There are many qualities in the people around us which we can learn to appreciate. God will give us the ability to recognize these qualities and genuinely to appreciate them. If we do not do this then our contact with unbelievers will be false and insincere. This will communicate that the only reason we want to be with them is to add another convert's scalp to our belt.

We are all capable of all kinds of sin. 'There, but for the grace of God, go I'. Jesus challenged the teachers of the law: 'If any of you is without sin, let him be the first to throw a stone' (John 8:7). It is not our job to judge. It is our job to show the way. God is the only Judge and his judgment is righteous. Ours never can be. When we are judgmental, we communicate a lack of acceptance. To the unbeliever we become unapproachable. We do not understand. We are different. We are living in another world. The example of Jesus is the perfect one. He loves *through* the sin, to the person underneath.

The choice is ours. If we want to be instruments of God to reach the lost, then we must learn not to be shocked.

Many people have asked me what to do when surrounded by bad language all day. It is an unpleasant thing to have to put up with, but bad language is so much a part of the unbelieving way of life that people use it without thinking. Christians have said to me, 'Ah, but blasphemy is different, using God's name, or Jesus' name, as a curse.' Here again I have to say that most people do not realize what they are saying. They do not realize that they are taking the name of the Holy God and using it as a curse. I know there may be some readers who will disagree with me and say that we should point out to the cursing unbeliever that we do not appreciate the name of Jesus being taken in vain. Fine, if that is what you feel you should do, then do it. I personally lean towards the full acceptance of the person and turning a deaf ear and a blind eye to what they do and what they say on the surface but giving all my attention to what they are.

I am a Christian. There are certain things that I do and don't do because I am a Christian. What I am determines my code of behaviour, just as what the unbeliever is determines what he or she does. It is ridiculous for me to expect someone without Christ to adhere to my code of behaviour. I have to accept that, otherwise I am going to run into difficulties of shock, judgment, criticism, frustration.

The same thing applies to dirty jokes. It is always difficult when a colleague opens with the line, 'Have you heard this one?' You know the feeling. Your heart sinks to your boots, you feel embarrassed, hoping it's not going to be too dirty, and wonder what on earth you are going to do and say at the end of it. There are, of course, various alternatives. You can get up and walk away, but that might be taken to mean, 'holy Joe can't take it'. Or you can sit it out and ignore it, and get on with what you are doing. That sometimes works. Or you can listen to the joke. If it's funny and just cheeky you can laugh. But if the joke is really filthy and refers very blatantly to sex, reducing the sex act to something base and animal-like, then we should not laugh or condone the joke.

I have said things like, 'I don't think much of that one I'm afraid. You're too nice a person to tell jokes like that.' And in that way, hopefully, I have attacked the joke but I still communicate my acceptance of the person who told it. Or another way is, as someone is about to tell a joke, to cut in and say very pleasantly or even jokingly, 'Is this going to be a clean one or a dirty one?' If the answer is, 'a dirty one', then say equally pleasantly, 'Do you mind if I don't listen, I really don't appreciate dirty jokes.' Whatever is said, we must never communicate a rejection of the person, only a rejection of the joke. Having said all that, there are times and circumstances in which we have no alternative but to listen. In those cases I can only say, don't communicate that you are enjoying it. Either don't react at all or simply do something else. Just do not attack the person telling the story.

I believe that we are going to see and hear far worse things than these before the battle is won. We are going to have to be mature about the nastiness around us. We must learn to take these things to God and ask him to keep our minds under his control. If our grip on the word of God is sure, then we have nothing to fear from the nastiness of the world.

Jesus was able to do the things that he did because he remained in close fellowship with the Father. There is our example. God will keep our minds through his word and he will enable us to move through this world freely without becoming contaminated and yet at the same time without blocking those vital channels through which we communicate the life-changing message of Christ.

# Get involved on their terms

I have already referred to this in the last chapter when I described some of the activities we can do to get to know unbelievers on their own ground. David was anxious to become a more effective witness at work. He talked to a friend about it who suggested that he could perhaps have lunch with his colleagues and spend the lunchtime break with them. David was horrified. 'No,' he said, 'their values and their standards are so different from mine, I don't want to be influenced by the way they think and also their language is very bad. I don't think I could put up with that every day.' End of conversation. David wasn't prepared to meet his colleagues on their terms. Not long after that conversation, he began to think seriously about changing his job in order to meet colleagues who were more acceptable to him as people and to whom he would 'more easily witness'. You can imagine that David never really did solve his dilemma.

The heart of the problem of the corporate communication of the body of Christ is that we have, for many generations, expected the unbeliever to meet us on our terms. We have tried to draw him into our fellowship and we have prayed that he would feel at home among us. We're surprised when he doesn't.

Jill was not a Christian. She recalled her first encounter with Christians. 'I remember very clearly being invited to a Christian meeting during a college lunch hour. I really don't know what made me go except that I had nothing else to do. From the moment I walked through the door, I felt very uncomfortable indeed. It was like walking into another world. I did not understand the terminology that the Christians were using in conversation with one another. I did not understand the speaker or anything that he was saying. I felt that he was directing all his comments to the in-crowd. Neither did I like the over-attentiveness of the Christians toward me. I felt suddenly smothered with affection and concern that seemed to me, then, totally false. Why should they suddenly turn this on because I had walked through the door of their meeting room when normal people just didn't act that way with one another? I sat it out until the end of the meeting and, needless to say, was the first to leave. I couldn't help thinking of the regular posters on the college notice board which insisted that 'all are welcome' to the Christian meeting. The content of that meeting was totally unwelcoming. The attitude of the Christians seemed to me to be a false kind of welcome, something they turned on because they felt they should. I vowed I would never go back.'

It is no use putting a poster on a board which in essence says: 'you are welcome to come into our little world'. We must be prepared to leave our little world and go out to theirs. Keep our lifelines strong, yes, our contact with God and with the fellowship, but we must leave the cocoon that protects us and get involved in the world.

Tony had just started a new job. He had been with his company about three months. Every now and again he had dropped a few 'tasty morsels' about his faith but had never entered a substantial conversation. So far things were going well and yet he felt he could perhaps do more to get to know his colleagues on their terms. An inter-departmental cricket match had been planned by the company and he was asked if he would captain his department's team. He was not a cricketer but as the match was going to be a fun one anyway, he decided he would do it. He admitted to me that he was not looking forward to it at all. He didn't want to make a fool of himself. That was one thing. But another was that he knew that after the match there would be a party with lots of drink and rowdiness. However, he decided that he would enter into the day wholeheartedly. His team played so badly that they came last in the contest but there had been a lot of fun, with people dropping catches, falling over and generally making exhibitions of themselves.

The party afterwards wasn't as bad as Tony had expected. In fact, he admitted that he had really quite enjoyed it. He went home feeling that he had done something to meet his colleagues on their level. In actual fact, he had done more than that. In the weeks following the cricket match, he noticed that his colleagues were different towards him. They were just that little bit more friendly. They were more open to him. They involved him far more in their conversations and the things they were doing. That one demonstration that he was willing to meet them on their terms established him as one of them. By some of the things that he had said previously, they had assumed that there was something different about him, but the cricket match opened up the communication channels totally. If he was prepared to make a fool of himself in front of the whole company, and prepared to have fun with them and go to their party afterwards, then he couldn't be too bad. He gradually began to win the respect of his colleagues.

We must be the ones to feel uncomfortable for the sake of the unbeliever. We must be the ones to take the responsibility of finding the level of communication. We must be the ones to take the initiative. It takes guts. It takes faith and sometimes a strong stomach, but it is worth it.

# Get them into the Scriptures with you

If, after the months – maybe years – of praying and building relationships, someone reaches the point at which they are ready to look more closely at the claims of Christ, then get them into the Scriptures. Only the Holy Spirit can convince someone of their need by opening the truths of Scripture to them. They need to see for themselves what Scripture is telling them. There are many excellent investigative studies for those people considering the claims of Christ, but have them do it together with you so that you can talk about it with them. Ask questions about the things that they have studied. Ensure that they do understand what the Bible is saying. The most important thing is that they understand the implications of the gospel before they make any kind of decision or commitment to Christ. By this I mean the fact that we are sinners and displeasing to God. The fact that we can never come to God except throught Christ. That we need a Saviour who forgives our sins.

These days, sin is a very unpopular word. In fact guilt is also an unpopular word. So many crimes today are rationalized as being the result of psychological disorder or emotional instability. There always seem to be reasons why people do the things that they do, and in acknowledging the reasons, our society often excuses to the point that the truth is ignored. So to talk of sin and one's own personal guilt with regard to our position before God is always going to be an unpopular proposition. How often do you talk to people who, in every other way, may be very close to giving their lives to Christ and yet they just cannot accept the fact that they are sinners and need a Saviour? They will say things like, 'But I'm not a bad person. I care about people around me. I don't do anything really wrong. Am I really that bad?' So it is important that someone like this sees for themselves from Scripture the truth of the separation that exists between God and man because of sin. 'Alienation' is a word that communicates this idea to many people today.

Of course we need to show that we understand. Yes, there are reasons why people do the things they do. We need to be aware of those. Yes, we need people and institutions to help us not to do those things. But more than anything else, what we need, each one of us, is a *Saviour*, and it is only when someone is brought to the point of realizing that they need a Saviour that they are ready to commit their lives to Christ.

It's often a long struggle. We go through many heartaches, many frustrations, as we are praying for our friends and waiting for them to entrust their lives to Jesus Christ. But it is God's battle, ultimately. He is the one who does the work. Someone once said to me when I was getting discouraged about my influencing others' lives, 'Val, you have God, the creator of all things, as your Father. You have a Saviour, Jesus Christ; you have the Holy Spirit and you have the word of God. That surely means that you have not only everything you could possibly need to be the person God created you to be, but also everything you need to do what he created you to do.'

He was right. I did. And I do. And so do you.